A SHORT GUIDE TO
POLITICAL RISK

SHORT GUIDES TO BUSINESS RISK, THE SERIES

Risk is a far more complex and demanding issue than it was ten years ago. Risk managers may have expertise in the general aspects of risk management and in the specifics that relate directly to their business, but they are much less likely to understand other more specialist risks. Equally, Company Directors may find themselves falling down in their duty to manage risk because they don't have enough knowledge to be able to talk to their risk team, in a sensible way.

The short guides to risk are not going to make either of these groups experts in the subject but will give them plenty to get started and in a format and an extent (circa 150 pages) that is readily digested.

Published titles

A Short Guide to Ethical Risk
Carlo Patetta Rotta
May 2010, Paperback, 168 pages, 978-0-566-09172-8

A Short Guide to Customs Risk
Catherine Truel
August 2010, Paperback, 144 pages, 978-1-4094-0452-1

Titles in production and development

A Short Guide to Kidnap and Ransom Risk
A Short Guide to Operational Risk

A Short Guide to Political Risk

Robert McKellar

Routledge
Taylor & Francis Group

LONDON AND NEW YORK

First published 2010 by Gower Publishing

Published 2016 by Routledge
2 Park Square, Milton Park, Abingdon, Oxon OX14 4RN
711 Third Avenue, New York, NY 10017, USA

Routledge is an imprint of the Taylor & Francis Group, an informa business

British Library Cataloguing in Publication Data
McKellar, Robert.
    A short guide to political risk. – (Short guides to business risk series)
    1. Country risk. 2. Risk management. 3. Investments, Foreign–Political aspects. 4. International business enterprises. 5. Business and politics.
    I. Title II. Series
    658'.049-dc22

Library of Congress Cataloging-in-Publication Data
McKellar, Robert.
    A short guide to political risk / by Robert McKellar.
        p. cm. – (Short guides to business risk)
    Includes index.
    ISBN 978-0-566-09160-5 (hbk) – ISBN 978-0-566-09161-2 (ebook)
    1. Risk management–Political aspects. 2. International business enterprises–Political aspects. I. Title.

    HD61.M387 2010
    658.15'5–dc22

                                                              2010021050

ISBN 13: 978-0-566-09160-5 (pbk)

Contents

List of Figures

① Introduction

OVERVIEW

International businesses face unique challenges. Most readers can relate from personal experience. When at home, we take most things for granted: we know how the transport system works; what prices and levels of service to expect when we go shopping or out for dinner; reasonable taxation rates and how much fudging we might get away with; which neighbourhoods to avoid at night; what kinds of behaviour will cause insult or charm; and the limits of the law's tolerance for our more eccentric behaviour. When we travel abroad for a vacation or business trip, even to countries with a broadly similar culture, this baseline knowledge needs to be partially abandoned and re-learned in the local context. We need to quickly adapt to new terrain, laws, and culture, and if we do not, then we become the hazard-prone traveller likely to have a very unpleasant, costly trip and come back more xenophobic than ever.

If we multiply the number of variables and the degree of complexity by several orders of magnitude, we begin to approximate the challenges facing large-scale foreign business operations.

Unlike their more home-bound counterparts, international businesses, those which have engaged in overseas environments in search of new markets, labour, and supplies, face an array of unique challenges. Different local and international regulations need to be taken into account; the social and environmental impact of any operation aside from only (and even then) trading will need to be considered; duty of care becomes more acute given that many staff are far from home at the company's behest; intercultural gaps and misalignments need to be bridged; the limitation or eccentricities of local infrastructure need to be factored into operational plans; health and safety standards need to be adjusted for a new climate; and HQ needs to manage the 'global–local' balance, or risk having an overseas office take on its own identity and strategy.

These are challenges that still confound even the most experienced international players, but even these questions presuppose a level of stability in the operating environment: The familiar 'rules of the game' still apply, however hard the game might be. There is another variable that affects international business operations, and which is more exogenous, less controllable by conventional business practices, and potentially more hazardous: political risk, the subject of this guide.

DEFINITION OF POLITICAL RISK

Political risk can be defined as potential harm to a business operation arising from political behaviour. The next two chapters will explore the issue at a historical and then theoretical level, but we can briefly deconstruct this definition for some conceptual clarity. We will address risk, harm, and political behaviour in turn.

Risk can be defined as potential harm, or hazard. More precisely, 'a risk' refers to a potential event or condition which, if realised, would cause harm or damage to a business. Risk is usually measured in terms of the probability of realisation, and the degree of harm, or impact, which would be incurred if a risk manifested. The intersection of these two independent variables yields the overall severity of a risk.

Three common errors in the interpretation of risk help to define the concept. One is forgetting that the two measures of risk (probability and impact) are independent. If something bad happens the effect might be disastrous, but if the chance of it happening is negligible then overall severity is limited. Conversely, just because something is nearly inevitable, it does not make it a severe risk unless the impact incurred would be relatively serious.

The second error is to equate uncertainty with a low probability. For example, if we have almost no idea about whether or not a risk will manifest, the best reflection is a probability of 50 per cent. This seems like a high score for something uncertain, but indeed it is the only accurate depiction of complete uncertainty: 'It could go either way.' Western intelligence services, as well as commercial risk consultancies, have long struggled with the question of whether or not to assign numerical probabilities to risk, but given differences in personal and linguistic/cultural interpretation of probability indications, a numerical assessment in conjunction with a descriptive indication is the safest bet.

Finally, there is considerable confusion about the difference between 'risk' and 'a risk'. Risk is negative potentiality, or the hazard incurred by being in a particular situation. A risk, as defined above, is a specific potential event or condition, such as a kidnapping or a scandal. We will be applying both usages. Risk as a concept is not the target of this guide, but it is useful to be aware of its implications, and some of the logical challenges it can pose.

Any business operation is ultimately aimed at achieving a specific profit; harm can therefore be defined as inadequate profit or loss. But focusing only on profit loses sight of potential harm to less tangible but equally critical factors of international success. For example, realised political risk can damage a company's reputation and thereby reduce a firm's moral influence with key stakeholders in a project. Another example is damage to the morale of key employees: Not only will performance on the ground suffer, but some international personnel might be reluctant to take overseas assignments in the future, thereby hindering a firm's capability to grasp overseas opportunities in the interests of long-term growth. Harm in our context, then, can be defined more broadly as damage to a business' capacity to succeed in overseas operations, whether in specific overseas projects or globally.

Finally we come to political behaviour. Politics refers to activity aimed at deciding how a society should be organised: who gets what and how; who decides on laws; and which prevailing ideals should be the moral basis for the social organisation (that is, a self-structured federation of groups who see themselves as part of a greater community, such as a nation-state). Politics occurs at a variety of levels. We most commonly associate such activity with states, but politics can also be global, regional or local. Another useful concept is political power: the ability to influence the social organisation. Governments often have official power, that is, the legal right to create and enforce laws governing society, but power can also derive from public mobilisation, economic bargaining strength, or raw coercion (as Mao wrote, 'Power comes from the barrel of a gun.')

Political behaviour is activity aimed at influencing politics, that is, maintaining or solidifying the status quo in terms of the social organisation; changing the status quo to align the social order with different interests or ideals; or influencing official power to further specific non-political economic or social interests (for example increased trade or labour flexibility). Such behaviour is undertaken by governments (or 'regimes' as might be more appropriate where official power rests more with specific individuals than institutions), but it is also undertaken by social activist and interest groups, insurgent and terrorist groups, transnational organisations such as the United Nations (UN) or the Organisation for Economic Cooperation and Development (OECD), and even the media when it has a particular political viewpoint. Indeed nearly any type of organisation, from a multinational company to an organised crime syndicate, can become a political actor if it actively seeks to influence politics. We must be careful, however, not to see everything as political. Ultimately the political arena is concerned with the social organisation and its underlying ideals.

We will apply these conceptual guidelines to help maintain focus, but there will be some inevitable stretching of these boundaries as we enter areas where politics and other spheres of life, and risk, begin to blur.

RELEVANCE OF POLITICAL RISK

The relevance of political risk derives in part from the fact that it arises from the interaction of two very different domains. First, a business exists to create profit for itself and its stakeholders, and business managers and investors across all sectors share a very specific language and mindset oriented around these objectives. Market share, growth, margin, and return on investment predominate in business thinking. A political actor, on the other hand, is concerned with the social organisation and its underlying ideals. The common language of political actors consists of authority, ideology, political culture and identity, the social 'good', and the levers of power to influence these. This distinction alone makes political risk a unique challenge to businesses, who need to understand at least the basics of a very different language and mindset in order to address it.

Second, the political realm is pervasive. Nowhere are we unaffected by the laws of the state, and indeed business occurs in a framework ultimately set by political authority and social consensus. In developed countries businesses can afford to take this framework for granted, since it changes very little over time. In many developing countries, however, the political domain is still evolving towards an equilibrium, and the framework in which business operates regularly shifts. Businesses need to adapt to a changing and often volatile political landscape, or they will find themselves at odds with the very ground on which they stand.

A third point of relevance is that the stakes are far higher in politics than business. If a business fails or disappears, it will not affect the lives of an entire society or nation. People seldom put their lives on the line to defend market share, but people routinely take extreme risks in seeking political objectives and death is often an occupational hazard for a committed ideologue. When an international business enters a politically volatile environment, they are exposed to often intense rivalries over which they have little control, and their interests will mean little to those engaged in the pursuit of their own political vision. Therefore political risk is arguably one of the most hazardous challenges that an international business can face.

Political risk, then, is relevant because it is challenging for businesses to understand, it is inescapable when dealing with developing countries (or emerging markets), and it is uniquely hazardous. All of these indicate the necessity of understanding it and developing competencies to manage it.

However, there is another reason why political risk is relevant. Some of the highest growth opportunities lie in developing countries, and globalisation is enabling and indeed compelling international businesses to seek these opportunities in order to maintain growth and competitive advantage. Yet political risk is endemic in such regions. There is a strong risk–reward equation in emerging markets. For those who can understand and manage the risks, the rewards will accrue. Political risk management, then, is a key factor for success in emerging markets, and a key enabler of international growth. Those who learn this competency sooner than others will gain strategic advantage, while for others political risk will remain a barrier to entry; they will watch their more adept competitors reap the rewards of emerging market presence, while established markets become ever more competitive and saturated.

OBJECTIVES AND SCOPE

The objectives of this guide are informed by a reading of the way in which even experienced international firms deal with political risk. Most companies regard their overseas operations in conventional business terms, and there seems to be an underlying assumption that the 'rules of the game' are more or less universal. Political variables are considered in standard Political, Economic, Social and Technological (PEST) assessments, but the political domain is generally not regarded as uniquely sensitive. In other cases, politics is often seen as analogous to the weather – it is an exogenous variable and its impact is largely beyond control. As with the weather, we can insure against the loss it could cause or we can avoid it, but actively managing it seems to be beyond the competencies that we normally associate with business.

Even when political risk is acknowledged as important and manageable, business managers are seldom trained in how to integrate it into strategic or operational decisions or how to apply corporate resources to mitigate it. Most managers learn by trial and error, and develop crude rules of thumb to guide them, often based on previous and perhaps inapplicable or unsuccessful experiences. Additionally, political risk management might be occurring in pockets within a firm or operation, but often in silos of activity which can easily end up working at cross-purposes.

Given the potential impact of the political environment in which international business operates, and the opportunities inherent in sound political risk management, an ad hoc and incoherent approach is far from optimal.

The aim here is to help provide a business-centric introduction to political risk, to familiarise international managers with the concept and to accelerate the learning curve towards proficient and coherent political risk management. At an introductory level, the book will address:

- the key political risks that companies have faced in the recent past, and current and future trends in the evolution of the political risk landscape (Chapter 2);

- the concept of political risk and its constituent elements at the analytical level (Chapter 3);

- models and approaches for assessing political risk in a specific global or operational context (Chapter 4);

- the principal options for managing political risk, and suggestions for organisational structures that could be developed to ensure a coherent and consistent approach (Chapter 5) and

- some of the wider issues that a company needs to consider in developing its own attitude and philosophy on political risk (Chapter 6).

As an introductory guide, the scope of the book is necessarily constrained:

- Political risk is most prevalent in emerging markets, as are the highest growth opportunities, therefore emerging markets are the principal geographic focus here.

- The focus favours operational and strategic issues, and less financial ones. The bulk of the current literature on political risk already tends to cover in detail project financing and insurance, and the risks best addressed by these measures.

- The focus is on political risk, not emerging market risk generally. There are others types of issues associated with entering emerging markets, such as health, crime, cultural and infrastructure risks, but we attempt to constrain ourselves to the political issues (there is some inevitable overlap with these other areas, especially crime).

- The book is necessarily an introduction. It is intended to illustrate the broad outlines of this complex issue and to provide a baseline knowledge of the subject to aid in further investigation; furthermore, there are diverse interpretations on political risk and this guide will inevitably have its own – further and diverse reading is recommended for a more detailed and holistic perspective.

(2) Political Risk: Continuity and Change

OVERVIEW

The objective of this chapter is to introduce some of the main political risks that international firms have faced, and to suggest how the global political landscape of business is evolving.

Political risk has been a significant factor in international business since the end of World War Two. Some challenges have been nearly continuous throughout this period, and can be regarded in some respects as 'background noise' at the global level, even if the political landscape might shift dramatically in specific locations. We will address these routine issues here and explain their effect on international businesses.

There have also been significant discontinuities in the global political landscape, especially in the last two decades. These macro-shifts have not necessarily changed the array of risks facing international business, but they have changed the character of several risks, and have made some issues much more acute. We will also examine these changes, and suggest how they have affected the nature of political risk now and for the foreseeable future.

This chapter elucidates political risk as generally experienced and understood by international managers. It introduces the issue at a common-sense and historical level. Chapter 3 will examine political risk in more theoretical and conceptual terms.

CONTINUITIES

As noted above, many of the politically driven challenges that international businesses face are not new, and at a global level have been with us for decades. Particularly to international business operating in developing regions, these represent the inevitable hazards of overseas exposure. This section will outline the key trends and conditions that have formed the 'background noise' in terms of risk in the global environment, and their general effect on businesses exposed to them.

INTERNATIONAL TENSIONS

Here we examine how tensions between countries can arise and their implications for international business operations.

Strategic and economic friction between national governments arises for a variety of reasons. There might long-standing territorial disputes that seem impervious to arbitration or even final resolution through armed conflict (as is clear in the Arab–Israeli case). There could be fundamental differences in national ideology, each of which regards the other as immoral or deficient (for example, the Cold War between the liberal-capitalist Western Bloc and the authoritarian-communist Eastern Bloc, or the current friction between Iran and the West). There could be cultural or historical differences which result in enduring mistrust (for example, the suspicion between China and Japan caused by Japanese imperialism of the 1930s and 1940s). It could simply be a matter of putting one country's self-interest over another's (as in many trade wars, or when disputes arise over treatment of each other's migrant workers and issues around their remittances).

Whatever the case may be, tensions between countries or blocs thereof can have profound consequences for international businesses. The adage 'the friend of my enemy is my enemy' can often apply. During the Cold War, for example, there were severe restrictions on the import of goods or services from either bloc, to the detriment of businesses and consumers alike. Arab–Israeli tensions still result in difficulties in doing business with both sides at once. Israeli goods are often boycotted in more hard-line Arab states, and business people who travel regularly in both Israel and Arab states are in for a hassle now and then. The US' long-running embargo on Cuba, to the extent of making it impossible for a business person to even travel to the US if they had significant dealings in Cuba plagued many firms facing potentially lucrative opportunities in Cuba but unable to risk making the US market inaccessible. Similarly, until quite recently Libya's significant oil reserves were inaccessible to firms unwilling to risk US ire. These are but a few examples.

Tensions can also disrupt supply chains, or make it impossible to use what would otherwise be optimally efficient supply lines. For example, rising tensions between the Philippines and Taiwan over Philippino migrant labour rights led to at least one period in which all transport between the two states was banned. This put severe pressure on several IT firms who regularly brought components from the Philippines to assembly plants in Taiwan. That same dispute has also caused even longer blockages of labour flows between the two countries, and this has impeded the long-term business planning of firms who rely on a flexible flow of labour to meet periodic demand hikes.

Finally, international tensions can result in severe restrictions in market access, either because of government tariffs (as in the US–Japanese trade wars), or because of state-sponsored consumer nationalism in purchasing trends (for example 'Buy American!').

International tensions particularly affect business operations which could significantly augment a country's national revenue and/or defensive capabilities, especially in a context of high strategic friction. Thus extractive industries, energy (especially nuclear these days) and aerospace and defence firms must tread especially carefully in conflict-prone regions. However, all firms with significant cross-border business face some degree of risk, albeit often at less dramatic levels, from international tensions in their global portfolio.

DOMESTIC UNREST

This section addresses friction and tension between competing socio-political visions and interests at the domestic national level, and how this has translated into challenges for foreign businesses operating in areas where such tensions give rise to intense political rivalries and direct confrontation.

Much unrest in developing countries can be traced back to the rapid decolonisation which quickly followed World War Two.

The result was that new states emerged, often led by ill-equipped governments prone to factionalism and in-fighting. The fact that many borders were arbitrarily drawn using the old European colonial boundaries, with little regard to real national or tribal homelands, made sub-national and ethnic conflict inevitable (that is 'We're stuck with these guys and they have control – if we don't do something they'll turn us into a virtual slave class or eliminate us within this territory.').

Even in states which had not been directly under the colonial yoke, such as in various quarters of Latin America, South East Asia and the Middle East, decolonisation represented a major and sudden loosening of European controls over domestic and regional politics, again resulting in localised struggles for political dominance. Political tension and conflict at the domestic level was a natural, and long-term, readjustment to the sudden change in control in all developing regions.

The 1960s and 1970s were rife with coups d'état, military intervention in politics, and low-intensity warfare between repressive regimes and insurgents. Africa was especially hard hit and experienced major wars aimed at sub-national independence (for example, Katanga, Congo; Biafra, Nigeria), but it was by no means unique.

The incidence of violent domestic unrest and confrontation has ebbed and flowed in subsequent decades, but it still remains a prominent feature of developing country evolution. Glance at a world map on a given day and any one of 30 or more distinct 'hot spots' come to mind, ranging from inter-communal and ethnic rioting, long-running insurgencies, military takeovers (Honduras, Niger, and so on), and spirals of tension between dissenters and repressive regimes (Iran, Turkmenistan and so on). It would be futile to provide a detailed list: Not only would it would be very long, but it could be outdated in even a few months.

International businesses operating in developing regions have always faced the risks inherent in civil unrest and domestic political violence: repression which affects their national workers and sometimes also expatriates; dramatic changes in foreign investment regulation brought on by sudden regime change; being caught inadvertently in locations where violence suddenly erupts; and becoming the target of sub-national insurgent groups who perceive foreign businesses as tacit supporters of a repressive or racist regime.

TERRORISM

Terrorism is the targeted use of force to cause maximum psychological impact on the enemy, and to inspire and mobilise political support through dramatic acts of rebellion. We will look at the recent history of the phenomenon, and how it has affected companies exposed to the global business environment.

Terrorism always seems like a dramatic new threat in any given generation, but it is in fact a centuries-old means of conflict most often utilised by political opposition groups who lack the means to directly oppose power-holders, but who perceive a reasonable probability that isolated spectacular acts of violence can weaken the opposition's political will, inspire supporters to resist the 'power', and neutralise potential antagonists by paralysis through fear. Since World War Two there have been four main types of terrorism which have afflicted international business; note that this is not meant to be an exhaustive list.

One is Red Terrorism, committed mainly by extremist off-shoots of European leftist movements and communist parties. From the late 1960s to the mid-1980s, these groups were a sophisticated, well-publicised but rather ineffectual threat to international businesses, which they perceived as agents of global 'capitalist-imperialism'. Their publicity was their main weapon: the chance of a business being directly hurt by such a group was remote, but given the media noise around the Reds' activities, it was inevitable that this strand of terrorism would become a major distraction and impediment to global growth. Collusion with Palestinian groups at times made the Red threat indistinguishable (see below).

National liberation insurgents seeking political recognition and sub-national autonomy in many developing countries also applied terrorist tactics not just against the state, but also against foreign businesses whom they perceived to be in collusion with the state by generating foreign revenues which aided the state's capacity to repress sub-national identities. The terrorists' analysis often is not far off – today major foreign investments are now scrutinised by government donor agencies and non-governmental organisations (NGOs) alike for their developmental impact, and their effect on peace and stability in terms of the risk of giving one side or the other in a conflict, usually the state, the upper hand.

The Palestinian Liberation Organisation (PLO) and its various off-shoots and splinter groups (the most notorious of which was the Abu Nidal organisation) saw Western businesses as colluding with 'Zionist' Israel through their perception of global businesses membership in the alleged pro-Israeli Western/US front. Palestinian groups collaborated with Red Terrorists to intensify the threat to international businesses.

Resources and theoretical rationales were often shared, and multiplied both the Palestinian and Red threat.

Finally, since the mid-1980s we have experienced Islamist terrorism, which is in effect a traditionalist manifestation of national liberation ambitions. Islamist terrorists perceive that secular ideologies from both the left and right have failed Islamic societies in terms of positive change, and postulate that politicised religion is a more culturally appropriate 'third way'. We will discuss this type of terrorism more in the next sub-section on change. Suffice to say that Islamist terrorists have readily perceived Western businesses, with their imperative of global expansion, to be agents of Western cultural and geo-strategic imperialism. As a result of this perception, Western firms have become a target set for Islamist terrorists, as exemplified most spectacularly in the Al Qaeda attacks of 11 September 2001, which mainly targeted the World Trade Center in New York, a hub of global business activity. Note as well the Bali bombings and the recent bombing of the Marriott in Islamabad: Western foreigners were a likely target set in each case.

How does terrorism affect an international business? First, and simply, it can, however seldom, result in the death and traumatisation of personnel, and this severely undermines not only immediate business operations, but also the stomach for international assignments among qualified personnel. Growth opportunities might exist in troubled regions, but not many people are keen to take on such challenges after even indirect exposure to hardcore terrorism (note again the gulf between political and business motivation – business is not war, and business people do not expect to be killed, as opposed to direct participants in a political conflict who see untimely death as an occupational hazard). In some rare cases terrorism can also destroy vital business infrastructure, as was plain in the 9/11 attacks, or the IRA attacks on the financial district of London in 1993.

Naturally, terrorism also increases the costs associated with duty of care, security, and employee/operational insurance. One large US construction firm operating in Algeria in the 1990s spent as much as 20 per cent of its annual country budget on security, most of it on anti-terrorist protection. As well, consistent terrorist attacks on any one foreign target can eventually portray a foreign business as an opponent of a national liberation struggle and/or as an agent of a repressive but business-friendly regime, however misguided, dramatised or unrealistic that interpretation might sometimes be. As improbable as terrorist-induced harm might be, terrorism is by nature unpredictable. We *might* get away with ignoring it, but we can never be sure that it will not one day affect us.

POLITICALLY-CONNECTED CRIMINALITY

In Casablanca, Bangkok, Rio, Nairobi or Dhaka, merely by way of broad illustration and to name a few of many potential locations, the unwitting tourist catches a bar of hash, or refined marijuana, from a teenager who throws it to the said foreigner. We instinctively catch this object to ensure that it does not strike our face and injure us. The local authorities miraculously appear, and *seem* to be upset by our having a sales-worthy quantity of illegal drugs. Jail-time in harsh circumstances accrues; pressure for a payback, often from uncoordinated and opportunistic elements within the alleged 'police', ensues. Much hassle and anxiety, on scant or baseless charges, is the fate of the alleged offender. This indirect payoff by criminals to the police benefits criminals by taking police pressure off their operations, and the police gain some extra, under-the-table revenue.

That is on an individual level, and draws on one of many situations in which criminality impinges on foreigners because they are foreigners, that is unwitting and lucrative targets. Companies endure the same kind of risk, and we can extrapolate from the above basic example to illustrate some of the challenges that international firms have faced.

Beforehand, however, the link between crime and politics should be made more explicit:

- In many developing regions, family, clan, community and gang ties link individuals in criminal groups to law enforcement or bureaucracy generally. Given the poor living standards in such regions, opportunities to pad mutually scant incomes and to help family or friends are often welcome. A combination of poverty, traditional social ties and lack of good governance is therefore often a formula for criminal–bureaucratic collusion, and foreign firms are wealthy and ignorant targets. In fact this phenomenon is not uncommon in developed countries either, with incidents of Mafia–state collusion in Italy being a prime example.

- In many cases the political will to enforce law fairly might exist at one level, but be lacking at another. For example, the judiciary or law-makers might be professionals but the police might be prone to corruption, or vice versa. In such cases, weak governance will likely prevail, and criminality of all types will increase, generally making the operating environment more hazardous.

- Governments lacking their own security resources sometimes rely on organised criminals as surrogate covert forces to pressure political opponents, and such pressure can be applied to foreign firms who do not readily concede to the terms of a government's commercial offer. A prime example of criminal surrogates was the 'Tonton Macoute' in Haiti – this was essentially a state-sponsored criminal secret society which acted as the right hand of the Duvalier regime which often called upon the group to enforce its will.

- Last but not least, when a government lacks oversight mechanisms and individual bureaucrats have the opportunity to build their own fiefdoms, there is an incentive for bureaucrats to insist on kickbacks or 'facilitation fees' for a given operation to proceed. In many cases said bureaucrats are the ones in the driver's seat when it comes to selection of the relevant foreign contractor. Such fees are in fact bribes, and the issue then is one of corruption.

The following outlines some of the main issues associated with this kind of risk; it is not intended to be exhaustive.

One kind of relevant white-collar crime is piracy (in this case referring to intellectual property rights infringement), which occurs through two processes. First, the foreign firm sells a product into a new market and criminals reverse-engineer the product and create their own cheaper version using the same or a modified brand. Second, foreign companies involved in infrastructure, energy or manufacturing operations import sensitive technology for their own use, and this is then stolen and reverse-engineered by local business partners. This risk is exacerbated considerably when legal protections for intellectual property are lax, or indeed when there is government collusion with the aim of accelerating national technical development.

Another white collar crime is fraud, wherein the foreign partner is defrauded out of ownership of shared assets or financial or brand control through illegal contract manipulation or subtle theft by a local partner. In each case, the criminals can succeed when there is sufficient support or wilful ignorance among the local enforcement agencies responsible for copyright infringement and contract enforcement (and these areas are hardly priority issues in many developing countries, where internal security tends to absorb most law enforcement attention).

The third major white collar issue is corruption, in which a government department, officials therein, or proxies thereof in state enterprises, demand a payment above and beyond operational and legal requirements in order to facilitate a given tender or execution of a project. This can be portrayed as culturally acceptable, normal, and necessary, and the project or country manager, under pressure to hasten the pace of business, is highly susceptible to this form of pressure. The company budget for such demands can be easily hidden in operating expenses, or as exorbitant but still 'normal' fees for facilitation/expedition/local consulting.

In the end most cases of gross corruption are discovered, often at the intense urging of aggrieved competitors but also from the watchful eye of home-country trade standards boards and host-country anti-corruption task forces. There are cases in which handing over a pair of Nike running shoes or a Nintendo set for a bureaucrat's children occur, or in which petty payoffs to an airport cop to help facilitate early and assured boarding of company personnel in very chaotic airports is not inappropriate – these exchanges are sometimes cultural and economic necessities and can be seen as interpersonal relationship-building and as personal favours in a situation where the 'rules of the game' are ill-defined. But gross corruption, in the tune of thousands to millions of US dollars, is not uncommon and very often incurs scrutiny which can lead to significant legal hassle and reputational decline of the perpetrating/participating firm and bureaucrat(s).

Extortion is a long-running issue for international businesses. A business person, or as demonstrated recently in waters off Somalia even an entire ship, might be kidnapped or seized for ransom or for public agreement with a political cause. A criminal group might also threaten a firm with fabricated scandal or violence if the firm does not pay a 'facilitation/protection' fee, or agree to a one-sided commercial relationship.

Kidnapping, a common form of extortion, is conceptually straightforward: a demand for money or public acknowledgement of a political cause in exchange for lives (and for goods as well in the case of sea piracy). It must of course be noted that nowadays in the Middle East and South Asia in particular sometimes kidnapping occurs purely in order to publicly execute a symbol of the opposing ideology, that is, a secular Westerner. In such cases the rules of the game change. Kindnap and ransom (K&R), consultants are better positioned to provide further nuance on this delicate subject, and such consultation is useful if firms are sending people to areas where extremist Islamist activity is common. There are other disturbing trends in kidnapping, such as 'Express Kidnapping' in Latin America as perpetrated by ad hoc and unprofessional gangs in search of a quick and dirty payoff; these trends should also be explored with the support of specialist advice. It is worth noting that kidnapping is geographically agnostic: Latin America and the Middle East/South Asia might be 'hot spots' now, but the phenomenon is not confined to these regions.

Scandal, another form of extortion, can involve tampering with a firm's goods or operations, thereby exposing local consumers or communities to risk, and then publicising the effect and blaming the foreign company, or making it look like a foreign firm has tried to circumvent local safety regulations. Scandal can be used against a foreign firm to weaken them vis-à-vis local competitors, but it can also used as a form of blackmail to compel a firm to abide with criminal interests. When a government is automatically inclined to favour local interests, it can be hard for a foreign firm to get a fair hearing or to go to local authorities for help.

Racketeering involving threats of violence, perhaps the most common extortion challenge, can begin with small-scale vandalism and harassment, which are then followed up with threats to the effect that problems will escalate if protection money is not paid. In developing states, it can be hard to know if the police would be able to help. They might be indifferent to the tribulations of a foreign firm, and at worst they might be in collusion with and benefiting from the racket.

Extortion operations can be crude, but are often beyond the apparent competence of local law enforcement, who could be well motivated to *seem* incompetent by access to a share of the criminals' proceeds, or when criminal and state interests converge (as is often the case in intellectual property crime).

WAR

War is a broad term, and especially in this era of asymmetric warfare it can be hard to distinguish war from periods of instability which include violent unrest and insurgency, terrorist campaigns, and so on. We will simplify the concept and define war as a state of open armed confrontation between different governments each yielding political control within its respective territory.

War can be between countries, but it can also be between sub-national groups (that is, civil war). In the latter case, war is often the end-point of an escalation of insurgency. The party fighting for a change in the status quo eventually acquires territorial control and legitimacy in a part of a country through low-intensity insurgency and terrorism, and then uses its territorial control to derive revenues, personnel and secure bases with which to fund, recruit and train a conventional military. It then wages open war with its original opponent, probably the current central government. For our purposes, the most important distinction between war and other modes of conflict is the element of competing, politically defined, territories, even if one side is not the internationally recognised government of an entire country.

A couple of examples might be useful. The Iran–Iraq War which raged from 1980 to 1988 was a classic international war. It was fought between two countries using all means of conflict but mainly conventional military force. Each government was the internationally recognised supreme authority in its respective territory. It began with the application of conventional and large-scale force, and by and large continued that way (albeit with periodic mutual use of terrorist tactics and Iraq's later use of chemical weapons, the now infamous yet elusive Weapons of Mass Destruction [WMD]).

Sri Lanka, on the other hand, endured until recently a classic civil war. It began with low-level insurgency and terrorism countered by state repression. Through low-intensity conflict, the rebel Tamil Tigers eventually gained control over a significant part of the country, and established their own government and conventional armed force. The war then became a largely conventional conflict between competing political territories, with the central government seeking to re-establish control over the whole country, and the Tigers seeking a formal degree of territorial independence for the Tamil community.

War has been a constant fixture on the global scene, and at any given moment dozens of wars are raging, however localised some might be. The effects for international businesses can be grave.

First, war makes potentially lucrative territories 'no-go' zones in terms of security and therefore restricts growth opportunities. It can simply be too dangerous to operate in or even visit a given city or country. In 1974, for example, Lebanon was a thriving international business centre in the Middle East and home to many regional HQs of foreign firms; by late 1975, any firm remaining in Beirut or other major cities faced severe peril.

Second, war can disrupt supply lines by making certain areas too risky for the transport of goods, or by disrupting the operations of foreign partners. Iran's attacks on Gulf shipping in an effort to constrict Iraqi oil exports during the Iran–Iraq War are a good example of risk to transport. Civil war in Colombia has often constrained the ability of local coffee suppliers to meet foreign demand (especially as many farmers were compelled to convert their land and labour to coca production to provide grist for narcotics exports which helped to fund both leftist and right-wing insurgent groups).

Finally, war can make it very difficult for a company to do business in or with one party or territory in a conflict without incurring the cold enmity of the opposing side. Oil operators in South Sudan in the 1990s, who were working on central government contracts, found themselves trapped between both sides in that civil war, sometimes with disastrous results in terms of local and international perception of their role in the war, and their own security on the ground. Periods of open war between Israel and neighbouring Arab states have intensified the long-running complications of trying to balance business interests in that region.

EXPROPRIATION AND CONTRACT CANCELLATION

For the purposes of a short guide, expropriation and contract cancellation can be treated together. Both are usually unilaterally carried out by a contracting government or state-owned enterprise, both result in non-realisation of profits through breach of contract or loss of control of a business operation, and both are predominantly legal and financial challenges. These are not dramatic issues, such as terrorism or war, but over the last few decades these issues have cost international businesses untold billions. First we will outline the concepts, then the triggers of these hazards, and finally their potential business impact.

Expropriation is often equated to nationalisation, which refers to a situation in which a government unilaterally assumes ownership of assets such as plants, land, and cash (the last via currency controls and unfavourable changes to profit repatriation regulations). Expropriation means broadly the same thing, but it is a more flexible term better suited to the current business environment, in which governments themselves are decreasingly the ones assuming direct ownership; rather it is increasingly common for governments to support efforts by local, normally partly state-owned enterprises to exert control over foreign assets. We will therefore use 'expropriation' here, but it includes and often manifests as nationalisation.

Another important distinction in recent years is the difference between outright expropriation and 'creeping' expropriation. The latter refers to a slow diminution of foreign control and ownership via incremental changes in the relationship with the government or its private sector agents. This is much more common nowadays, because multilateral trade guarantees or political risk insurance schemes backed by major country or transnational lenders (for example, the US Overseas Private Investment Corporation [OPIC] or the World Bank's Multilateral Investment Guarantee Agency [MIGA]) easily recognise outright expropriation and will often readily act against it, whereas incremental adjustments in a bargain, however unfair, are often relatively unnoticed by all but the foreign firm itself. Creeping expropriation is therefore much harder to guard against, and is therefore preferred by potential perpetrators.

Contract cancellation involves a government or state-owned enterprise unilaterally cancelling a contract with a foreign firm after the contract has been signed and in many cases even partly implemented. It can result in or include expropriation of foreign assets, though this is not always the case.

There are several triggers common to both challenges; these include, though are not limited to the following.

First, a new regime comes to power or expands its grip on power (either by democratic change, coup d'état or manipulation of controls on the power of the executive), on the premise of fighting corruption and elitism. In order to shore up its new authority it needs to quickly deliver on its promise of 'taking from the rich to give to the poor' and of exerting control over national assets on behalf of the 'people'. Foreign firms are wealthy and often hold or control national assets, but they are still subject to national law and government decisions, and are thus ideal targets for early wins in terms of delivering on a platform of people-power.

One classic example of this phenomenon is drawn from Iran in the early 1950s, when the radical Prime Minister Mossadegh sought to nationalise US and UK oil assets in Iran on the premise that the old imperialists were reaping profits at the expense of Iran's economic future (his threat to nationalise assets is generally seen as a major factor in the US/UK-orchestrated coup against Mossadegh in 1953). A more recent and well-known example occurred in India in 1995, when a newly elected government in the state of Maharashtra (the new government was mainly comprised of the Communist Party) cancelled a contract with a US power contractor on the basis that the deal was fundamentally at odds with the long-term interests of the people. After considerable renegotiation the contract went ahead, but on far less profitable terms for the foreign firm.

Currently this phenomenon is occurring in Venezuela, led by the leftist Chavez regime: The government has threatened several foreign firms with nationalisation if contracts are not modified to give more control to the government. Many of Chavez's threats have not been carried out, but they still play havoc with longer-term planning.

Another trigger of expropriation or contract cancellation is sheer self-interest among social groups or indeed individuals who have considerable sway with the relevant level of government. In these cases, social elites or members thereof will exercise their political influence in order to safeguard or enhance their self-interest, usually at the expense of the foreign firm.

One example occurred in Indonesia in 1996. A UK petroleum firm, the main stakeholder in a local joint-venture, had a contract to produce refined petroleum products which required ethylene as key ingredient. The government insisted that a local ethylene manufacturer be utilised, but there were few choices, and the principal local producer demanded above-market prices. The UK firm refused to pay the asking price, arguing that it was cheaper to acquire the ingredient on the global market. In fact the Indonesian president's son had a major stake in the local producer. The Indonesian government ended up raising tariffs considerably on ethylene imports, thereby making the local product cheaper than global imports and compelling the UK firm to acquiesce to local provision, with a significant hit on profits. Although this is not a clear case of expropriation, it is a case of creeping expropriation, wherein the state-sponsored side gains control over an operation by increments. This case is drawn in part from Louis T. Wells' contribution in Theodore H. Moran's *Managing International Political Risk* (Blackwell, 1998) p. 16.

Another example is the case of a US constructor working on water infrastructure in an underdeveloped South American country in 2000. The US firm was to modernise and then, for a set period, operate a new water distribution system on behalf of the local water authority. The modernisation was successfully carried out, but the deal had included differential consumer water rates, according to consumption levels – this was a change from previous nearly flat rates as defined by household or facility. The wealthy classes, who were also owners of agricultural land, had been using water exorbitantly. When the new tariff scheme was introduced, there was an uproar among the heavy users, who happened to own much of the local press as well. They saw their water rates sky-rocket, and they used their public relations clout to vilify the foreign contractor as allegedly trying to privatise and take over water supply in order to effectively hold the entire state at ransom. After eight months of controversy culminating in street riots protesting foreign control of the water supply, the state government was quite ready to cancel the operating phase of the contract and throw out the US firm. This is a highly nuanced case and remains open to interpretation. Again, examples abound, but the above are hopefully illustrative.

A very recent case involved a joint venture between a UK and Russian oil firm in Russia. After increasing friction, the head of the UK element was sent packing, in what seems like a state-sanctioned effort to increase control of the Russian element which seems to have had significant stakeholders in the government.

A third suggestion for why expropriation or contract cancellation occurs is simply a perception that a foreign firm really has been acting unfairly or against the real interests of the host country. This can happen on a variety of levels: unfair profit-sharing; excessive control of scarce national assets; abrogation of labour rights; and outright cultural ignorance or insult. We can call this set of reasons aggrievement. A perception of unfair deals and excessive foreign control was, for example, the principal reason behind the Chilean Allende government's plans to nationalise US business assets in the early 1970s (interestingly, this too led to a coup d'état in which a pro-US regime came to power, with alleged collusion on the part of affected US firms).

It is difficult to pinpoint modern episodes in which aggrievement has been the sole factor in expropriation or cancellation. Rather, it is often a contributory factor, and it provides the moral basis for government intervention. Governments and their state-owned commercial elements also often leverage or indeed cultivate any sense of grievance to justify what would normally be illegal encroachment on a foreign firm's stake.

The net effects of expropriation and cancellation are wasted time and investment; direct loss of financial and physical assets; in some cases legal liability if a government charges that it cancelled a contract because of underperformance; and reputational damage that comes from association with well publicised embroglios. The friction surrounding such events can also put company personnel at risk, as they become pawns in a high-stakes game and directly face the wrath of the host government, which might well apply its criminal connections or covert pressure to seek acquiescence to 'an offer you can't refuse'.

BUREAUCRATIC MORASS

Most readers will identify with this issue from personal experience. We all know how much paper we deal with each month, and the experience of being surprised by regulations that went unnoticed (for example, our gas bill was much higher than expected because we did not read the fine print, and so on). Companies end up in the same situation, and where the 'rules of the game' are still in the process of definition, there are two main issues.

One is the lack of definition of specific permissible actions. For example, in the 1990s a foreign contractor needed to import industrial saws into Algeria. It bought them in France, then shipped them under what it thought was the appropriate label to Algeria, only to find that the authorities had labelled the same goods under another category, one in which some parts, in this case the blades, had to be made locally. New blades then had to be locally sourced, the blades and saws shipped back to France for reassembly, and some weeks later the assembled saws arrived back in Algeria. Unforeseen delays were the result.

The other issue in a developing country is lack of coordination between agencies governing foreign direct investment. The final set of regulations that arrive in the hands of the foreign firm are often rendered only by the department or ministry in closest proximity to the foreign firm's operation. These notices can be useful, but they often lack nuances that indicate requirements among subordinate or peer ministries. Operations could well be held up because the full chain of approval is not understood and complied with.

Red tape manifests in a variety of ways, and depending on the level of coordination between relevant government departments can be elusive and time consuming. Knowing all the relevant requirements for a specific operation is one way to mitigate this risk, but ensuring that there are no contradictions between the requirements is more difficult. What this means for the foreign firm is quite clear: delays which put contract or business performance at risk. This appears to be a rather mundane area of risk, but it has accounted for very considerable hassle and delays in foreign operations.

LEGAL UNKNOWNS AT THE INDIVIDUAL LEVEL

We have all likely had the experience of learning about a legal nuance after it is too late to save us from having committed a minor infringement. This can happen in our own back garden. When a staff member has been assigned to a foreign environment, where laws are even more opaque and we are less accustomed to limits of official tolerance, this risk is multiplied considerably.

Here is one example. A company manager operating in a North African country understands that his local partner needs anti-virus software in order to be able to safely integrate relevant systems with the foreign partner. The manager in question authorises a few thousand dollars for transfer to the local partner to enable purchase and instalment of the security tool. Local authorities, who are running a 'Transparence' (transparency) campaign learn of the transfer and, having been ardently looking for examples of corruption, arrest both the foreign manager and his/her local counterpart on corruption charges. The arrangement for providing the software funding was never really committed to paper in detail, and as such it is easy for the authorities to allege that the payment was a kickback, punishable by law. Considerable hassle ensues, even though both original parties to the arrangement never had any nefarious intentions. Perhaps in a few months the transparency campaign ebbs of its own accord, and all is forgotten. Perhaps not.

Here is another potential example. A foreign subsidiary experiences the death of a worker, foreign or local, through criminal activity. The company at group level looks into the death for potential abrogation or duty of care, and the home country government is also interested in the case. But the local laws are much harsher. The country manager is arrested on the basis of negligence and held indefinitely until the case goes to trial or guilt is absolved.

Both cases serve to illustrate that local law not only needs to be considered, but can be surprisingly different from home country law, and in developing countries is often opaque and transient. Abiding by strict rules of engagement which seem to cover all potential abrogations and keeping written documentation on deals and arrangements is one way to reduce the risk, but at times, especially in the context of fluid international business dealing, this can be onerous. Suffice to say that foreign operators need to be cognisant of legal differences and eccentricities. It can be very hard to extricate someone from a legal quagmire once it has engulfed them.

ETHICAL CRITICISM

Ethical scrutiny of foreign business operations is a relatively recent phenomenon. It has grown with the role of civil society, the degree and pace of information exchange, and a decline in Cold War tensions which has led to less acceptance for the 'national security' imperative for not questioning international developments which might previously have had an underlying geo-strategic rationale. It is a 'political risk' because the aim of those conducting ethical scrutiny is often policy change aimed at greater regulation of international business, and/or shifts in the underlying ideological basis of international business – that is, away from raw pursuit of profit towards more responsible corporate global citizenship.

In the 1950s such scrutiny was more or less proscribed by Cold War paranoia and the national security imperative. It was acceptable to criticise the other bloc's moral weaknesses but not one's own side. In the 1960s ethical criticism blossomed, especially in the US and Europe, but there was much hyperbole driven in part by the rejection of the rationales for the Vietnam War, and by general rejection among educated youths of the hegemony of the 'ruling class', that is, the grey-haired white men who held power and resisted new perspectives and ideals. From then on, ethical scrutiny became more sophisticated, driven in part by diminutions in the Cold War, and by information technology which made it easier to globally publicise localised infractions of human rights and environmental standards.

Since the mid-1980s ethical scrutiny has tended to be well informed, relatively balanced, and tenacious through self-confidence. It is also much more effective through professionalisation, technological sophistication, and greater awareness of how businesses operate.

Ethical scrutiny of international businesses now focuses mainly on:

- Environmental concerns:

    - Is a business operation or a company's line of business a potential cause of irreparable damage to the ecosystem?
    - Is an operation likely to jeopardise sustainable means of livelihood, or the livelihoods of indigenous peoples who already exercise considerable respect for their local ecosystem?

- Human rights:

  - Does a business operation require the abrogation of human rights, as defined by the UN or other relevant transnational organisations, in order to succeed (that is, do people need to be repressed as a function of business continuity)?
  - Are sub-national groups or indigenous people going to be marginalised or have their cultural identity diminished as a result of a given operation?
  - Are local labour forces treated fairly and in line with international labour standards?

- Economic justice:

  - Will a business operation support improvements for the entire populace, or is it likely to result in advantages for a narrow set of interests at the expense of others (and this includes gender as an interest set)?
  - Is a business operation going to provide benefits by way of long-term and sustainable development, or is it likely to make a country or sub-region dependent on a specific and perhaps tenuous sub-sector (for example oil, minerals, or specific consumer/industrial goods) controlled by the foreign investor?

- Conflict sensitivity:

  - Will an operation impinge on tensions in a country or between countries? Is an operation likely to increase the probability or intensity of conflict?

- Corruption:

  - Does a company rely on bribery to facilitate its operations? Has bribery been a factor in winning a tender or sustaining an operation?
  - Has an operation undermined good governance in the host country?

The principal actors posing these questions and trying to ascertain the answers would mainly be NGOs such as Greenpeace, Amnesty International, the International Crisis Group, Transparency International, and also larger domestic NGOs in developing countries. They will likely collaborate with and voice their concerns to relevant transnational organisations (TNOs) such as the UN, World Bank, and so on. Together, NGOs and TNOs will try to ensure that national development agencies, such as the United States Agency for International Development (USAID), the Department for International Development (DFID) – UK or the Deutsche Gesellschaft füe Technische Zusammenarbeit (GTZ) – the German Agency for Technical Cooperation – will recognise and support their concerns. They in turn will try to affect foreign and trade policy of their respective governments. Finally, all three sets of actors will likely campaign to raise awareness about ethical concerns among international businesses, as well as their home-country populations, which of course encompasses shareholders and customers.

Examples of ethical criticism having an impact on business operations abound. Just recently a major US oil company working in a Central American state has found itself at the receiving end of an expensive lawsuit alleging gross infractions of environmental regulations and corruption. In 2000 a mid-sized oil firm was forced to abandon lucrative operations in Sudan through shareholder activism and NGO-instigated lawsuits alleging government human rights abuses committed using company facilities (helicopter pads) with the knowledge of the foreign company. Numerous fashion companies have faced allegations of using sweatshops in developing countries to cheaply manufacture goods which are later sold at exorbitant margins in developed country markets. One result has been consumer activism, that is, the boycotting of goods made by alleged perpetrators of labour abuse.

Importantly, ethical scrutiny is not levelled just at the controlling firm, but also at its entire supply chain. A consumer might buy a basic commodity, say a hammer, from a respectable brand and long-standing outlet. A concerned NGO is likely to look at where the hammer came from, and to identify ethical issues in the total supply chain: where did the parts come from; were labour rights adhered to; was the product or its components made with an eye to environmental sustainability; and so on. It is not enough to say 'We didn't know.' A company is now expected to know and to some degree control where and how components and final products or commodities originate.

In Chapter 5, 'Political Risk Management', we will delve into more detail on how companies can actually mitigate the risk of ethical scrutiny. There are a variety of international standards which a firm can subscribe to and measure itself against in order to reduce real or perceived ethical breaches. Suffice to say at this point that this challenge has become very germane to operational sustainability and especially reputation, and is one area of risk which is more under a firm's control than several others, such as war or instability.

CHANGE

The above-mentioned challenges have been with us for decades and will likely remain issues into the foreseeable future. But there have been some very significant changes in the last two decades which have altered the nuances of political risk, that is, its sources and intensity. We outline the main ones here, and briefly explain how they have affected the hazards of international exposure.

POLITICAL ISLAM

The rise of political Islam is one significant shift. Until quite recently, for decades the primary axis of global ideological contention had been between left and right, as manifesting in the Cold War and its various proxy conflicts. Islam has of course had never been apolitical (as with most other major religions, for example, even allegedly pacifistic Buddhism is a source of political identification among Sinhalese in Sri Lanka), and indeed even since World War Two there had been manifestations of Islamist influence on politics. But 1979 marked the point when Islam came onto the world stage as a third axis of ideological tension. The Iranian Revolution of 1979 was the culmination of decades of slow-burning anti-regime sentiment among myriad classes and interest groups. The Shia clergy, best organised and with the broadest support base, came out on top, and steered change towards an Islamic Republic, with much repression of alternative strands of revolutionary thought.

The reverberations of this event went far beyond Iran. People in predominantly Islamic countries and sub-regions across the world saw that there was a 'third way' to combat political stagnation, corruption, cultural depletion and repression, and

POLITICAL RISK: CONTINUITY AND CHANGE ②

Iran was more than keen to assist newly empowered Islamist revolutionary groups in realising their aim of turning over old orders. Iran intervened directly in the war in Lebanon, primarily supporting Hizbollah in its efforts against the Israelis and local secular and communal opponents. It also helped long-repressed Gulf states' Shia populations to manifest their grievances via armed dissent, and assisted Hamas in Palestine in its development as a major political contender. The influence of the Revolution also coincided with Islamist rebellion in Egypt (as manifesting in the assassination of Sadat by Islamists in 1981, for example) and the beginnings of Islamist dissent in Algeria which ultimately led to a direct electoral challenge to the pro-West military regime in 1988, and subsequently, after a military coup in 1991–1992 aimed at thwarting Islamist ambitions, to become a brutal and drawn-out civil war between Islamists and the secular state.

The Iranian Revolution was one cause of the rise of political Islam, and perhaps the lynchpin. But US, Arab Gulf, Pakistani and Iranian assistance to Mujahedin guerrillas in Afghanistan during the Soviet occupation (1980–1988) also helped to bring the phenomenon onto the world stage. Islam was the principal rallying cry for aggrieved Afghans under the Soviet yoke. Islam went beyond mere tribal politics and warlord-ism and unified vast swathes of the population against the secular invader. Thousands of youths from across the Muslim world enlisted for service alongside the Mujahedin. The legacy of this war was a hardened cadre of Islamist fighters who later partook in the contemporaneous war in Lebanon, and new wars in Chechnya and the Balkans. The legacy also included the founding and definition of Al Qaeda, once an amorphous Arab group dedicated to funding and logistical support for the Mujahedin, subsequently to become a hard-core rebel group unto itself. Small and secretive though it might have

41

been, through moral influence and skilful use of the Internet it became the principal head in a global hydra of Islamist ambition and militant activism.

The Soviets were scared. Many of their southern Republics were predominantly Muslim, and the Afghan war had seen high desertion rates among Muslim Soviet soldiers. The US was not scared for a long while. With US support, the Islamists helped to beat the Russians out of Afghanistan and appeared to be allies for a time, despite the on-going rift with Iran and Hizbollah attacks on Western bases in Lebanon. In the 1990s, after the collapse of the USSR, that was all to change, and Western–Islamist differences were to culminate in the Al Qaeda-sponsored attacks in the US on 11 September 2001.

Nowadays the Left is not defunct, yet it is now but one of several global ideologies competing with Western liberal-capitalism for influence in the developing world. In the Muslim world, radical political Islam has largely replaced the left as the main rallying point for angry youth and middle class, who see little hope for their future in defunct and repressive pro-Western regimes.

Unlike the old enemy, the Soviets, Islamist terrorists do not play by the rules of diplomacy nor recognise limits in their means to achieve an end. After all, they have few bases which can be attacked, their leaders are easily replaced by ever more radical ideologues, they have little to lose, and no fear of the afterlife. Radical political Islam has thus become a significant nexus of ideological contestation with the West, and is sure to be a source of terrorism and insurgency unfriendly to Western, and Western business, interests for years to come.

COLLAPSE OF THE USSR

Another major change in recent decades has been the collapse of the USSR and its control over Eastern Europe. The why and how of this collapse are nuanced and beyond our remit here. Suffice to say that the USSR's economic system was hindered by over-centralisation. The state had taken on the role of provider and could not derive revenues from private or alternative sources (which it had subsumed) to sustain this role. What it spent it took from itself. This became unsustainable especially given its self-imposed isolation from the mainstream global economy. In the 1980s the war in Afghanistan and the Reagan Administration's intensification of the arms race added to the burden, and the USSR, under the pragmatic (or defeatist) Gorbachev caved in. Hegemony over Eastern Europe collapsed in 1989, and the USSR itself imploded in 1991.

Naturally the West, the US in particular, was jubilant. The strategy of containment had worked; it had kept the bear in its cage long enough to starve it into submission. But jubilation was short-lived. It soon became apparent that the demise of the old enemy meant the rise of myriad other concerns.

First and foremost, the old Soviet arsenal was still intact, but no longer under central control. Who controlled the nuclear weapons? How would they use their nuclear know-how and material? Are material and knowledge secured?

Second, the new ex-Soviet republics experienced the same syndrome as newly-unfettered nations in the post-colonial era. Border and ethnic wars and the rise of repressive regimes ensued with little delay, especially in the Caucasus and Central Asia. There were indeed the 'coloured' revolutions, notably in Ukraine and Georgia, which brought a semblance of democracy to the fore, but these did little to ease the overall instability of the ex-USSR.

Next, loosening security in the old USSR and Eastern Bloc unleashed a wave of organised criminality, hardened and expertly elusive after decades under harsh repression (and now in collusion with many KGB officers left unemployed by the changes).

Finally, after the post-dissolution dithering of the Gorbachev regime and the absurdities of the Yeltsin era, Russia finally got tired of being a global joke. Putin gained the reins in 1999, and his cold and uncompromising demeanour was a stark reminder that Russia was still a power to be reckoned with, and not subject to the whims of the West. Russia has reasserted itself as a global power, and its arms industry continues to supply not only itself but second-tier burgeoning states around the world with sophisticated and dangerous weaponry.

Western businesses saw considerable opportunity in the fall of the USSR. It meant the opening of previously closed markets, supply sources and supply chains, and the spread of business-centric ideals. But it has opened a Pandora's Box at the same time. The new markets are often less than business-friendly, local competitors often do not abide by the 'rules of the game', and the prospect of global conflict has been replaced by an increased probability of regional conflicts, and the intensification of conflicts beyond the old USSR through a conversion of conditional arms transfers to opportunistic arms sales.

In addition, the old Cold War used to keep regional conflicts in check. Each side supported one regime or the other, and either Bloc's influence often sustained regimes that would otherwise have collapsed into anarchy. Without the heavy hand of the Cold Warriors seeking to counter each other in proxy conflicts, many defunct regimes have been left to their own devices, only to flounder and add to the problem of failed or failing states (see later in this section). The implosion of the USSR might have been inevitable and might ultimately be globally beneficial. For the time being, however, it creates as much confusion and risk as opportunity, and optimism needs to be tempered with considerable caution.

GLOBAL MULTI-POLARITY

Another recent and significant 'about face' on the global scene is the manifestation of multi-polarity. The Cold War enforced a bi-polar world: 'You are with us or against us.' With the demise of the USSR, burgeoning powers no longer had to cater to one side or the other for economic and military support. China in particular saw its role in the eastern hemisphere blossom as a result of the Soviet demise, and it is rapidly becoming a global superpower unto itself.

The 'New World Order' as envisioned by Western ideologues in the early 1990s has in fact given way to a new Babel, for better or worse. The US and its NATO allies might still wield the best means of power projection, but especially with over-extension in Iraq and Afghanistan they are loath to take on new powers, and even smaller powers which could be problematic (for example, Iran and North Korea). Even Russia, for several years regarded as a defunct country in search of external mentors, has firmly reasserted itself and is often at odds with Western interests. On a purely economic level the list of contenders is even larger, and includes at least India, Brazil, Korea and Indonesia. Japan too is realising that it has more potential on a geo-strategic level than it has exercised in the past, and is increasingly beginning to look out for itself.

Mapping and predicting lines of international tension has thus become more challenging than at any point since World War Two. The opportunity afforded by new markets and supply sources is often countered by the unpredictability of the global landscape and the need to account for myriad foreign interests, not just a handful as previously defined by the bi-polar order. As well, the advantages of being a 'Western' firm are fast eroding. With an equalisation of state power around the world, state backing for global business enterprises is also equalising. For example, the Chinese government's assistance to the international expansion of Chinese firms has already had a significant impact on the balance of international competition, often at the expense of Western businesses. There is opportunity in the New World Disorder, but there is also need for adjustment to a new and more diverse playing field, and more potential international friction points that need to be managed.

FAILED AND FAILING STATES

Another significant anomalous trend has been the manifestation of 'failed and failing' states, partly another outgrowth of the end of the Cold War. As noted above, one consequence of the Cold Warriors no longer having to uphold proxies in the developing world has been that fragile regimes have been left to their own devices. In several cases this has led to political implosion and near or virtual anarchy, either across an entire state or in parts thereof. This is not a new phenomenon: Where the US or USSR had little interest previously, they were happy to let things go awry. Haiti is a case in point, as well as several states in Africa. But the phenomenon has intensified since the end of the Cold War.

When a state collapses, it effectively becomes an unregulated, unpoliced and unobservable territorial entity. And one thing that international insurgents or criminals need is a safe base in which to collect their thoughts and lay down sufficient roots for equipage, recruitment, indoctrination and training of new recruits, safe from the watchful gaze of an internal security apparatus which might have previously reported to one or the other Blocs. These territories can then become staging grounds for global operations which harm the citizens and interests of established power centres, and generally increase entropy at the global level.

To apply a broad-brush approach, there have typically been two kinds of failed/failing state. One kind is riven by internal power differences and civil war, which eventually falls into a situation where there is no effective central government but several competing sub-territories or sub-factions. Afghanistan is the most well-known case. Other current cases include Somalia, at the extreme end, and parts of Burma/Myanmar, the Democratic Republic of Congo, Yemen, Chad, and north-west Pakistan. Such examples tend to give rise to, and attract, ideological extremists who find some local empathy with their cause, whether ethnic 'national liberation' or global political Islam.

The other kind manifests through extremely weak governance and social fragmentation. There might not be any discernible competing territorial parties, rather myriad politico-criminal gangs and a fragile, isolated central government, itself likely to be just one more self-interested party. Examples include Haiti as mentioned earlier, Guyana, Papua New Guinea, and in the last decade several West African states including Liberia and Sierra Leone (though in the latter cases with international support the situation has improved). In these cases, criminal groups have often manifested, creating in effect a mafia or 'narco-state'. The above is indicative and there are more examples, and more nuance, under the rubric of failed and failing states.

In either case, the results for international businesses have been not just severe risk in trying to operate in such areas, but an intensification of terrorism and criminality at the global level. Al Qaeda is a good example of how state failure can increase global risk. After Bin Laden's Afghan escapades during the Soviet invasion, he became alienated from the Saudi regime and sought refuge in a very weak, although not quite failing state, Sudan, where he had considerable support among more extreme elements of the regime. Through Western and Saudi pressure he then had to leave, and Afghanistan, then a failed state under tenuous Taliban control, was an open field. He had to pay his way via funding and logistical support for the Taliban, but because of shared ideological inclinations the prevailing power let him stay with few questions asked. The Taliban likely would not have welcomed him if they had known that he would use their country as a staging ground for an operation which would incur the full wrath of the US and its allies upon their own heads, but the situation was sufficiently nebulous that he could do so without much inhibition.

Even if a company assiduously avoids failed and failing states, their wider impact on global stability, and by extension business security and continuity, will be a challenge. This particular bend in the road has only just begun to manifest.

GLOBAL ASYMMETRIC WARFARE

A further shift in the geo-political landscape has been the accelerated development of global asymmetric warfare capabilities. Asymmetric warfare means that opponents of established political systems have an unusually high capability to cause injury to states (including citizens). It effectively means more 'bang for the buck'. For example, if a Western power had wanted to destroy a major economic centre in another country, the operation would have involved hundreds of planners, analysts and technicians, and the utilisation of expensive aircraft and munitions, probably to the tune of tens of millions of dollars if not more. Al Qaeda operatives achieved the same result in the 9/11 attacks on a budget of around a million dollars. This phenomenon is as old as war itself, but it is now more dangerous and more global in scope.

It has become more dangerous because the illegal trade in sophisticated weapons and ingredients for bombs and chemical weapons has more than kept pace with demand; many non-weapon military technologies have become freely available on the open market; failed/failing states enable terrorist groups to plan and train for major attacks with relative impunity; and the current fad of suicide attacks means that terrorists do not have to take the survival of their operators into account – they therefore can penetrate more deeply into sensitive target areas.

The phenomenon has also globalised. Previously, insurgent warfare was often conducted within one geo-contiguous territory in which lines of communication and logistics were defined by physical access. The Palestinians and Reds in the 1970s broke free of these constraints to an extent, and were able to operate at the global level, but even then international operations depended heavily on the cooperation of sympathetic states.

Nowadays, the Internet and all related technology that has been developed to make life easier and more efficient for businesses and individuals has also provided insurgents with the means to break free of physical bonds. Instructions alone, with a basic knowledge of paramilitary skills, suffice to extend an insurgency to the global level. Another enabler of globalisation is the widespread use of traditional and nearly untraceable international fund transfer mechanisms, such as Hawala or Hundi, as often utilised by Islamic groups.

The current and likely future of the asymmetric warfare threat includes a higher probability of the use of weapons of mass destruction, attacks on critical infrastructure, a higher incidence of very destructive suicide attacks, and the formation of loose federations of like-minded militant groups joined by sophisticated electronic communications. Cutting the head off the opponent means little when dealing with a hydra.

This phenomenon of course ties in with Islamist terrorism, and with the phenomenon of failed or failing states. Islamist extremism is the first ideology to fully utilise all modern global assets at hand, the Internet in particular, and failed states accelerate terrorist activities considerably by providing at least limited safety from which to plan and train.

Islamists are not the only ones to benefit from trends in technology and globalisation. Any modern insurgent group relies heavily on the Internet and related information technology for coordination and transfers. Recently, for example, a rebel leader in Colombia was captured along with his laptop, and it is arguable which was more useful for the state intelligence services.

How the state and society counter such threats is an ongoing debate. Certain 'rules of the game' are emerging, and perhaps ironically physical force is not among the priority means. The threat, however, has emerged more quickly than countervailing doctrines and force structures, and as such is going to remain a concern for years to come.

CURRENT INDICATIONS

The baseline risks combine with recent shifts in the global business landscape to create a unique era in political risk. Any effort to succinctly capture this is doomed to lack of inclusiveness, but we will still try to define the current issues in a brief snapshot that will at least inspire consideration of the full picture. What, then, are the emerging issues for international businesses? We can suggest these hypotheses:

- Increased ethical criticism. Modern global communications make it easy for ethical observers to share and coalesce information about corporate breaches in ethical performance, to coordinate well-informed critiques, and to publicise such critiques for a mass audience.

- Increased confusion in terms of inter-state tensions. The range of potential global disputes and power centres has multiplied, and while international businesses might be pursuing raw profit, aggrieved states will not see it that way when a business takes more interest in an opposing state than themselves – the company can be seen as an international player whether it likes it or not.

- Increased exposure to civil violence. The demise of the Cold War and more recently widespread state failures have led to the creation of a range of new 'hot spots', each of which has its own eccentricities, and pursuing apparent opportunities in such locales incurs exposure to unpredictable regimes and the propensity for localised regional conflict or civil unrest.

- Increased exposure to terrorism, a threat accelerated by the rise of Islamist extremism, failed/failing states, and advances in asymmetric warfare. The terrorist threat once fitted tidily into the upper left of a risk grid, that is, improbable but high impact, but recent shifts in asymmetric warfare place the terrorist phenomenon more to the right. Now it is *moderately* probable and has even greater impact.

Thus we have a snapshot, but any concerned reader should regard the above not as a definition of current risk, but as a starting point for a more in-depth understanding of the issues. And we reiterate that the baseline hazards remain alive and well. The full risk picture needs to take into account the whole legacy of risk, not just recent 'hot' topics.

(3) Political Risk: Analytical Variables

OVERVIEW

Chapter 2 introduced the reader to at least the key trends in political risk, and some of the baseline and recent issues that businesses face in the global environment. However, it can be difficult to identify political risk relevant to a given firm or operation unless we know the constituent elements of the phenomenon, and which issues and questions to focus on. This chapter breaks political risk into manageable sub-elements. This not only helps in understanding the subject, but also begins the process of generating hypotheses on priority risks in our specific context. This chapter addresses: the relationship between business sector and relevant types of risk; the concept of risk tolerance; the assets that we expose to risk in volatile environments; the sources of political risk in a given environment; and the different levels of political risk in terms of geographic scope.

BUSINESS SECTOR AND APPLICABILITY OF RISKS

Risks faced by a company depend to an extent on the business sector a firm competes in. This can be a useful starting point in defining the broad types of risk relevant to specific business contexts. We will provide a few illustrative examples here of how one's sector can incur different types of risk.

Companies in the consumer sector, for example, rely heavily on brand and consumer loyalty, and on cheap overseas inputs and labour. They therefore face greater risk of brand fraud, supply chain disruption, and consumer activism based on ethical fault-lines in sourcing or supply chains (for example, use of child labour or sweatshops which becomes a political issue as presented by interested NGOs).

Companies involved in heavy industries, for example, large-scale industrial manufacturing, extractives or infrastructure, need to implant themselves in their operating environments for a number of years for any one project. Their presence can cause considerable disruption to host environments. They also often work on state contracts or with state partners. They thus face greater risks from on-the-ground opposition to their engagement and control, from host government-led initiatives to attenuate that control, and from localised unrest and conflict.

Another set can be called the 'controversial sectors'. These include firms which make products to address basic social needs, such as medicine/pharmaceuticals or potentially critical agricultural products (for example, genetically modified seeds for all-weather production). Such firms can be seen as exploiting these needs and seeking to profit by controlling access to fundamental social goods. It also includes firms who meet the demand for unhealthy habits (for example, tobacco and alcohol), who can be regarded as seeking profit at the expense of health and well-being. Finally, it includes suppliers of armaments and military infrastructure, who are often perceived as recklessly endangering humanity in the pursuit of profit, and as active players in international conflict. Such industries face especially acute ethical criticism and regulatory control by dint of the controversy surrounding the nature of their business.

While business sectors overlap in terms of risk, a useful starting point in identifying relevant issues, especially at the corporate level, can be a consideration of what the fundamental business sector really is, and the repercussions that this entails in terms of exposure.

RISK TOLERANCE

A second factor in the consideration of political risk is how much risk a company is willing to bear. There are situations in which risk consultants tell clients, 'This operation is clearly unfeasible because you would have to put people at risk, and it could well backfire in terms of your reputation with key stakeholders', and so on. And the client company replies, 'We're aware of that, thanks, but our people know the risks and we have no option but to engage, or we hand over a key opportunity to our competitors.' Assessing risk and being aware of the hazards is critical in all cases, but what risk means to a company depends on its own aspirations and limitations.

Risk tolerance is a factor of the competitiveness of the business sector – the more intense the competition and the higher the stakes, the higher the willingness to take risks. It is also a factor of a company's culture; more entrepreneurial firms are sometimes willing to take higher risks than those used to more level growth trends.

Unfortunately, risk tolerance can also derive from a cavalier attitude amongst key players in senior management, who might advocate a culture of 'cowboy-ism' in order to grasp all possible growth opportunities whatever the risk. These days, with high duty-of-care standards and high liability for firms who underperform in this respect, companies cannot allow a few individuals to set the benchmark in terms of risk. Risk tolerance needs to be an agreed company-wide standard with ample room for exemptions for individuals whose personal situations do not leave room for much risk-taking.

Setting the level of risk tolerance is necessarily an explicit exercise that takes into account all of the above except the 'cowboy' culture which is inevitably found among some old international hands or the hyper-ambitious. Whatever the agreed benchmark might be, there needs to be space for open dissent, personal exemptions without career penalties, and flexibility in the face of changing circumstances.

WHAT IS AT RISK

CRITICAL ASSETS

Any given operation or line of business will have its own unique range of critical assets, that is, those attributes and possessions which enable successful international business to occur. For example, a consumer goods company relying on exports for growth will be very concerned with reputation and brand. A heavy projects company, such as in the construction or energy sector, will be more concerned about personnel and on-the-ground business continuity. Nonetheless, for all cases, three general types of assets apply: people, reputation, and performance. Across sectors or operations the mix and emphasis will vary, but understanding these three general types of assets will help managers to develop hypotheses on their own unique firm or operation's exposure.

PEOPLE

People are a critical asset in more ways than one. First, it takes time and resources to select, train and inculcate people within an organisation. They then become the bedrock of the organisation's cultural identity, itself a key entity which ensures continuity of performance and fulfilment of external perceptions. Second, the way in which a company looks after its people is often regarded by external stakeholders as indicative of its commitment to business principles and sustainability. A firm which regards people as expendable (usually in the sense of layoffs and quick 'fire and hire' cycles, but in more extreme ways in terms of unassisted exposure to high-risk environments) is often regarded as a fly-by-night operation unworthy of serious investor or partner attention. Finally, people ultimately make things happen, and their morale is fundamental to performance. If people feel valued, they give back in turn; if they feel as though they are regarded as expendable, then they will be hesitant to invest themselves in a dubious employer.

All three aspects of the value of people (identity/brand continuity; reputation; performance) are undermined when someone, or several people, are hurt, traumatised or demoralised by political risk. How can political risk affect people? The following are some of the more common possibilities:

- Direct trauma, death, or injury. The issues range from the subtle, gnawing anxiety of dealing with corruption or political pressure, to panic incurred through the physical/ logistical inability to escape emerging unrest, to direct harm incurred through exposure to conflict; business people have experienced the full set. People can be hurt, but whether or not violence is involved, people can be left with serious psychological trauma and an unwillingness to take on even minor risks in the future.

- Demoralisation through watching colleagues go through the above-mentioned issues, or through knowing that such trauma regularly befalls co-workers.

- Distrust of the employer based on increasingly routine exposure to risk without requisite preparation and knowledge, and through pressure to perform even in high-risk environments without recourse to say 'No thanks', or to ask for more appropriate resources to manage new or intensifying risk. This kind of distrust can also arise between country operations and corporate HQ when the country office feels that HQ is ignoring or downplaying risk faced by country personnel.

A good example of personnel risk, and its consequences, derives from the experience of a Western firm operating in Algeria in the mid-1990s. Several staff needed to get to the operating site deep in the Sahara, and for reasons unknown decided to go overland. The security adviser was a foreign ex-policeman with limited exposure to unstable environments. The team proceeded south, and during a stop in one town well-known for the presence of Islamist rebels, the team was ambushed. A few people were killed. The survivors hid in the local police station. HQ and relatives were anxious as a result of delayed contact, but no information was forthcoming – the team had no satellite phones. It was a couple of days before the situation was understood, and before country HQ could provide support. This episode led to a complete revision of security policy, but unfortunately still made it much harder to recruit qualified international personnel to the Algerian operation.

People are indeed the bedrock of any business initiative, and any consideration of political risk must put people at the top of the list of priorities. With a full knowledge of the issues, an often welcome open door to abstain from risk exposure, thorough preparation for work in unstable places, and solid planning to take care of people in the worst of circumstances, people will align well with a firm's growth aspirations in unstable regions. If people are regarded as expendable, then growth can only happen by far-flung and tenuous local relationships in which the firm has little real control over its operation.

REPUTATION

A company's reputation can be defined as its character as perceived by key stakeholders, including owners/shareholders, staff, investors, partners and the societies in which the firm operates (the latter including NGOs who monitor business ethical performance, and the media). Reputation gives a firm moral gravitas and credibility, which in turn can be major sources of influence when seeking support for business initiatives. Without a solid reputation, getting support of key stakeholders is a constant uphill struggle, and business performance will suffer.

Political risk can affect reputation in several ways:

- Political actors hostile to the firm can use their public influence to vilify the firm, and potentially orchestrate scandals that make it appear as though the firm has been ignoring social needs or underperforming.

- A company can become trapped between political interests who have divergent expectations of the company. For example, a contracting authority might want to see a project go ahead as quickly as possible, while a local NGO will be watchful of the firm's respect for the environment and social needs in the host community – the net result can be conflicting efforts to please which are probably going to leave the firm open to some criticism by both sides.

- If a firm does not properly identify its political and social stakeholders, and does not proactively respond to their concerns, it can appear insensitive to social interests, and incur severe criticism and bad publicity which reaches not just other willing critics, but eventually regulators, partners, customers and shareholders.

- Reputation can also actually be harmed by a *perception* that a firm is unable to manage political risk. If a firm incurs risk to personnel or performance, it appears to be unable to deal with complexity and is often regarded as a lame duck in the fast game of emerging market expansion. Potential partners and investors will be wary of firms who tend to get into trouble.

An all-out reputational blow-out is the worst-case scenario. One well-known example is a mid-sized foreign oil firm operating in South Sudan in 2000 (previously alluded to – see Chapter 2, p. 27). The company relied partly on the Sudanese military for its security, even though the army was at the time heavily engaged in the civil war with the South (Note that the facts of the case remain under debate). At one point the army apparently asked the firm if it could park helicopters on company property, and the company agreed. The helicopters were in fact gunships, and allegedly flew punitive missions from the company base, with disastrous results for nearby villages.

Company staff on the ground apparently raised questions with HQ about the reliance on a military regime antithetical to the interests of the surrounding community. HQ was allegedly intransigent and sought to proceed regardless. Watchful NGOs activated their media networks, and company shareholders rebelled. The company in question was taken to court in North America by activist groups representing shareholders. The case remains an embarrassment. The company sold its Sudanese assets, and now assiduously avoids terrain where ethnic conflict might become a factor in operational performance, even areas where risk, by global standards, is only moderate. This has limited market access in some potentially lucrative areas and growth initiatives remain conservative.

Reputation can suffer in a number of ways as a result of manifested political risk, and the above examples are only indicative. The main point that a reader can take away is that although reputation is an intangible asset, it is a critical one, and is vulnerable not just to political risk but also to mismanagement thereof.

PERFORMANCE

Performance is to some extent a factor of people and reputation, but in the short term these other variables are not necessarily critical. For instance, in both examples above, the companies in question were well on track with their business objectives, and remained so even after they incurred harm to personnel or reputation. Manifested risk in those cases had longer-term, albeit very serious implications. Performance, on the other hand, refers to the routine meeting of business and project targets, hence its treatment as a separate asset.

Business performance can of course be divided into a number of sub-factors, but in the context of political risk it refers primarily to continuity and control. Continuity means the ability to keep operations on track in the face of a high-risk operating environment. This means the ability to identify and avoid risk, and to efficiently mitigate risk when it manifests, thereby ensuring that the effect on day-to-day business is minimal. Control means the ability to maintain ownership and influence over an operation, even when there are political pressures (for example, from state-owned enterprise partners) to relinquish ownership or decision authority. Continuity without control might yield results, but the foreign operator will not see the full benefits of its own performance. Control without continuity is equally fruitless – control over a stalled or intermittent operation is often more hassle than it is worth. Both are fundamental to the performance equation.

Continuity is highly vulnerable to unforeseen political changes or to localised political tension. Supply chain linkages can be disrupted because of international tensions; regulatory instability can lead to the need to hack through new layers of red tape in order to facilitate imports of critical supplies or expatriate personnel, or to renew operating permits; unrest and conflict can lead to 'lock downs' wherein staff cannot travel safely to and from work and need to remain at home for extended periods, and can lead to temporary evacuations which incur lost project time; local political disputes can lead to labour or social activism which impedes day-to-day operations, and can lead to vandalism or sabotage/theft of key physical assets, such as plant machinery or trucks. In the more extreme cases, political turmoil can lead to a long-term cessation of operations when the operating environment simply becomes too 'hot'.

Control (as we saw in the sub-section on expropriation in Chapter 2, pp. 27–32) can often be tenuous. It is nearly inevitable in a developing country context that the state or state-sponsored partners will increasingly seek control over an entire operation in which the foreign partner is a key player. The foreign partner brings high-value technology, machinery and knowledge to a country desperately seeking to acquire new means to development, and appropriation of some elements of these is often an unspoken state imperative.

If a contract is not designed with an eye to this risk, foreign firms can find themselves giving away more and more knowledge and control as an operation proceeds, in the worst cases to the extent to which the foreign firm loses its bargaining power and becomes redundant or irrelevant to local partners and the host government. At that point a company should be able to extricate itself with a semblance of profit, or renegotiate terms towards a more favourable balance of influence, but more often than not such cases result in the choice between a loss of control, or a legal quagmire and mutual bad feelings which impede not just the immediate operation, but also future work in the country or region (not to mention lost profits and liability to the charge of under-performance).

Continuity and control are two halves of the same performance coin, and both are vulnerable if risks are unnoticed, treated in blasé fashion because they initially appeared to impede new opportunities, or left unmitigated. A firm that cannot perform in hard circumstances is vulnerable not just to earning a 'lame duck' reputation, but also to underperformance in the context of obligations to itself and its stakeholders.

SOURCES OF POLITICAL RISK

We have an understanding of how different business sectors are exposed to different types of risk, risk tolerance, and the critical assets that are most affected by political risk. All are necessary in terms of deriving hypotheses about the most urgent issues facing a foreign operation.

Another set of variables that is useful in deriving pertinent political risk is where it comes from: the underlying conditions that generate political risk. Risks themselves will seldom be immediately apparent, but the sources of political risk are more readily accessible to the trained or conscientious observer, and can serve as indicators in terms of risk identification in the context of a specific firm or initiative. There are three broad sources of risk: political instability, weak governance and conflict.

POLITICAL INSTABILITY

Instability can be defined as a persistent serious challenge to the legitimacy and longevity of a government. Political dissent occurs all the time everywhere, but in developing countries in the early stages of political development there are two preconditions which make it much more serious.

One is little to no separation between a specific executive leadership and a government. The ruling party or regime tends to permeate and tightly control many major political institutions, and therefore any challenge to the leadership is automatically a challenge to nearly the entire system. For example, in the UK, if someone disliked the government's current policies, they would say they wanted the present administration to collapse or be replaced. You would seldom hear 'We want the UK government to fall.' In a developing country, it might be very unrealistic to believe that things could change just by changing the immediate executive leadership. The whole government therefore bears the brunt of dissent, and clearly there is more significant change and trauma associated with challenging a government than a specific ruling party or clique.

The second precondition is a lack of legitimate channels for dissent, such as a free press, regular fair elections, an independent complaints/human rights commission, the existence of an active and independent political opposition or even basic freedom of expression. If a group wants to seek changes in government policy or attitude, the only recourse then becomes illegal activity, which is likely to be met by a heavy-handed government reaction against what is officially criminality. This reaction, which probably includes violence or detentions, is likely to further inflame discontent and delegitimise the regime. A spiral of increasing dissent and repression can be the result, and the stakes become higher with each round. The spiral can be contained for a while by severe repression, or stabilised by periodic compromises, but its ultimate logic, if unchecked, is violent regime change, with much chaos on either side of this transition.

Challenges to the government can come from outside of it, led by organised protest groups and, at later stages, insurgent groups. This is what we usually see, because it is more visible. External regime change often takes the form of a revolution, that is, a major revision of the government in which the old slate is wiped more or less clean. Even in a relatively quick and bloodless revolution the end result can be messy, as different groups who were united in protest against the old government are suddenly left without a common aim, and vie for control of the structures of power and compete in establishing their own social visions as mainstream.

But challenges can also come from inside the government, from cliques within those institutions that the ruling regime has not brought firmly under its control, or even from factions within the regime itself. As internal dissenters prepare themselves for a transition, there can often be a long period of 'shadow government' during which internal dissenters create a covert sub-structure as the mechanism for ultimately carrying out a power transition, usually through a coup d'état. In many countries new to democracy, the military, long the most established and professional element of government, will maintain a certain level of preparedness for political intervention, to be enacted if the civilian government fails in providing effective leadership or diverges too far from the original binding social vision of the nation.

The results for international firms operating in areas where instability exists have been highlighted in common-sense terms in Chapter 2, but to reiterate, these are likely to include: a high incidence of violent protests and unrest which endanger personnel and impede operations; repression, often affecting local personnel; insurgency, often involving the use of terrorism; policy stagnation or reversals as the friction between different power factions impedes effective governance; and sudden regime change followed at best by a period of ambiguity and heightened repression, and at worst by an increase in unrest as the 'winners' vie for control of the vacuum they have created.

WEAK GOVERNANCE

Weak governance is another source of risk. We have discussed the issue above in terms of the potential inability of a political system to accommodate dissent, but the issue of governance has more facets. Weak governance can be defined as inept, unprofessional, or negligent leadership and management across a broad spectrum of governing institutions, though usually starting at the top, that is, the ruling regime. We see it in developed countries to varying degrees, but in developing countries it can be much worse and endemic, for two main reasons.

One is simply a lack of resources and experience. Many developing countries are poor, and cannot afford the training, education and technology that underpin good governance. They are also still quite new, in historical terms, to the concept of the modern nation state as developed and imposed by colonial powers, and the Western model of government tends to compete with previous modes of governance, such as tribal, religious or caste-based rule, or consensus decision-making by leading representatives of semi-autonomous sub-national groups (for example, the 'Loya Jirga' in Afghanistan).

Another reason is the persistence of personal rule, that is, the dominance of a small clique of key personalities who regard their position more as a privilege than as an official duty, and see political institutions as their own tools for exercising control. In effect, when political institutions are weaker than the personalities governing a country, the whole system is prone to human error and human eccentricities.

Personal rule arises partly from a lack of experience or familiarity with the nation-state concept, wherein political institutions exist independently of a specific ruling party or leader. When institutions are weak, people can in fact feel more confident in having well defined personalities at the helm rather than rely on nebulous officialdom to make law and allocate resources in society. Personal rule also arises from opportunism and raw ambition on the part of those capable of taking power. There is no more powerful or advantageous a position than running the country, and when political institutions are weak, it is relatively easy for the power-hungry and influential few to dominate a government. It is then in their interest to keep political institutions such as the legislature or judiciary weak, and to repress political debate, to avoid official or legitimate challenges to their power.

Note that the above makes no comment about the difference in political ethics between developed and developing countries. In any country where institutions are too weak to prevent the rise of personalities, personal rule is likely to manifest. The West need look back no further than World War Two to see one of the worst instances of personal rule the world has ever experienced, and the issue has periodically raised its head in developed countries to varying degrees since.

The effects of weak governance for international businesses include: arbitrary policy reversals; personal and unexpected intervention in contract negotiations; a lack of rule of law and shifting regulations which makes the firm and its personnel subject to unanticipated legal charges and liability, and which necessitates a regular relearning and renegotiation of the legal and regulatory environment; shifting and arbitrary red tape in obtaining operating and import permits; pressure to engage in corruption or the preferential treatment of partners or suppliers close to the regime; and official collusion in politically-connected crime.

CONFLICT

Conflict is the final source of political risk. It can be defined as friction between highly divergent interests and social visions. Unlike instability, wherein risk arises from a steady build-up of dissent, conflict is inherent in the character of the antagonists, who often perceive their relationship with each other as a zero-sum game, that is, winner takes all. Conflict is often preceded by a build-up of tensions over time, but it ultimately manifests as an 'us and them' attitude which makes conciliation very difficult, and in some cases apparently impossible.

Conflict manifests at several levels. A country or bloc may see another's economic or strategic gain as directly detrimental to its own interests. It can manifest between different sub-national groups or ethnicities within the same state, when there is a perception that another group's gains are losses to oneself (Rwanda is an extreme case). It can arise at the end-point of a spiral of instability, when tension between dissenters and the government reach a point of no return, and each side sees its own survival in the other's complete defeat or eradication.

There are also several axes, or sources, of conflict. One is economic interest, wherein a scarcity of resources compels one side to jealously guard and expand its own gains even at another's expense. Another is competing visions and ideologies, wherein one set of values is antithetical to another. And it can arise during periods of high insecurity, when one side sees strategic control over its environment and other groups as fundamental to its own survival in the face of chaos and uncertainty.

At the international level, for an international firm conflict means: political sensitivity and hostility incurred from operating in a rival country or bloc; international war with consequent risks of violence and supply chain disruptions; trade wars and disputes which impede the free flow of products, labour and materials; and international terrorism. At the country level, the effects of conflict include: civil violence as rival sub-national groups clash; domestic terrorism usually as part of a sub-national insurgency; severe repression; and civil war, which results not only in violence but possibly violent and chaotic regime change.

THE INTERACTION OF THE THREE SOURCES OF POLITICAL RISK

Each source of risk can exacerbate the others, and they work together to generate a range of political risks which cannot necessarily be attributed to a single source. For example, instability is intensified when the dissenter/government axis aligns with ethnic conflict (that is, the regime and dissenters are mainly comprised of different rival ethnic groups). Instability is also intensified by the personal rule aspect of weak governance, which reinforces the need to challenge the whole government to effect a change in leadership. Weak governance in turn impedes effective responses to conflict and instability, and often makes conciliation or concession beyond the capabilities of a regime even if they regarded it as desirable or necessary. Any specific risk, then, could derive from or be made more acute by inter-linkages between the different sources.

Nonetheless, knowing what these sources are is an indispensable starting point in estimating what risks might be relevant to the company or operation. When we know that a given source is present and acute, and what risks it can lead to, we can begin to develop hypotheses on the specific issues we might face, after which a more nuanced analysis can reveal the linkages and likely reveal additional challenges.

We should note before concluding this section that we did not provide a specific source of risk for ethical criticism or company friction with political stakeholders. This is because such issues derive as much from a company's behaviour and how it handles political risk as from the environment. A fourth source of risk, if we need to label it, would be the company's own lack of competency in political risk management, but as this is under the company's control it is not taken forward as an analytical variable. The issue of how reputational risk can be exacerbated by certain conditions is addressed in Chapter 4.

LEVELS OF POLITICAL RISK

The final consideration in developing hypotheses of political risk relevant to one's context is the level of analysis. There are three: global, country and operational.

GLOBAL

An international business is exposed to risk wherever it operates, and wherever its supply chains exist. A company therefore needs to be aware of risk at the global level, in terms of broad regional risk trends, global issues which cut across all or several regions (for example, international terrorism), and the global regulatory environment. A country or project manager might find a global assessment to be quite irrelevant, but from the point of view of corporate planning, especially in terms of growth and market expansion, a holistic view of global political risk can be invaluable in assessing opportunities and balancing the global portfolio, that is to say the full set of geographic growth opportunities ranging from low-risk/low expected returns, to high-risk/high expected returns. It is not uncommon for informed planners to gaze at a world map, weighing potential initiatives against what they know or sense is happening in different parts of the world.

COUNTRY

Country-level risk is relevant when a firm has a major operation in a specific country, or when a certain country or sub-region is high on the agenda in terms of anticipated growth. Country analysis usually examines the situation in absence of specific operations. The key question is, 'What is going on in this place, and what are the key risk trends?'

This provides a baseline awareness of risk which can then be applied to specific operations, and augment global assessments.

OPERATIONAL

Risk at the operational level means the issues that arise from the interaction of a specific initiative and presence on the ground with the surrounding political environment. Clearly a country-level assessment is useful in mapping risks to a specific operation, but typically operation-level assessment will be far more contextualised and localised. Country-level politics are relevant, but even more so are local politics. How does the surrounding community perceive the operation, what are the local conflicts that could be exacerbated by the presence of the operation, who are key local stakeholders and how do we get them on board, what are the risks of hiring from any given ethnic group or community, and how can we be as fair as possible? As one international manager put it, operation-level assessment is about 'Whom do I drink tea with?'

Defining the appropriate level of analysis helps to narrow down the issues we face. At each level the other two will be relevant, but the more specific the assessment to a given set of business decisions, the more effective it will be. In subsequent chapters for the sake of parsimony we will often merge the country and operational levels, but analysis specific to each level can be applicable.

SUMMARY

This chapter has been relatively academic, but necessarily so. We have broken the wider concept of political into: business sector and risk; risk tolerance; assets at risk; sources of risk; and levels of analysis. Knowing each of these helps to put parameters on risk assessment and management, and importantly helps to generate initial hypotheses about relevant risks.

Starting with the bottom-line question, 'What are our political risks?' is seldom feasible, and can yield some pretty fantastic and incoherent results. Initially asking broader questions about each sub-element of political risk is more manageable, and ensures that key questions are addressed along the way without leaping to conclusions based on supposition or a general reading of what kinds of political risk exist. The next chapter will utilise these elements in a holistic fashion to indicate how political risk can be reasonably assessed by international managers whose principal concern is enabling global growth and overseas operations.

(4) Assessing Political Risk

OVERVIEW

The objective of this chapter is to provide insights into how political risk assessment (usually synonymous with 'analysis') is conducted with the aim of deriving actionable conclusions to shape risk management strategies. How this chapter's insights are applied would be subject to the individual reader's position and remit. For analysts and consultants, it could augment or adjust an already established approach. For senior business managers, it hopefully provides sufficient benchmarks to scope assessment needs and guide the process, and to evaluate the analytical rigour underlying assessment conclusions.

There is an array of approaches to political risk assessment, and different types or levels of analysis use different approaches. One common offering by political risk and country analysis firms is comparative risk ratings and future risk estimates for a range of countries. These are usually based on complex predictive models of instability and a government's inability or unwillingness to fulfil contractual obligations. These have a place in top-level analyses of a firm's overall global portfolio (which we examine later) and in defining the risk factor in investment decisions. There also are reasonably successful attempts to incorporate political risk as a factor in the logic of investment decisions using sensitivity analysis and other methods. Another common technique in political risk estimation is the Delphi method, so-called through reference to the ancient Greek Delphic oracle. The assessing actor defines questions about the future of political risk in a given operating environment, and asks several experts in that environment (for example, consultants, journalists, academics, diplomats and so on) to briefly answer the questions. The assessor would then use these as inputs into an overall inter-subjective estimate.

These, and more, all have their place and the reader should research the possibilities. However, in keeping with our focus on political risk as a manageable variable, in this chapter we look at an approach which helps managers to make actionable decisions about risk mitigation. Generally speaking, there are as many models and approaches as there are problems, and few, if any, are 'proprietary'. We attempt to define or capture a few models here which lend direct insight into political risk management requirements.

There are three stages of analysis at both the corporate and operational levels: contextual analysis, which defines the factors by which we derive initial risk hypotheses and interpret risk; risk analysis, which derives priority near-term issues; and scenario analysis, which examines how the risk environment might change in the future. We will deal with each stage in turn.

CONTEXTUAL ANALYSIS

There are two kinds of contextual analysis specific to the corporate level. One is its tolerance to political risk, that is, how willing the firm is to subject itself to the common risks incurred by exposure to unstable emerging market environments. This helps the company to decide whether a given growth strategy or overseas initiative is acceptable or too risky in its own unique context. The second is its current global political risk portfolio, that is, a map which correlates our global exposure and political instability across our operating environments. This enables the firm to balance the risk–reward equation in international growth planning – too much exposure and the firm is vulnerable to strategic disruption, too little and the firm might not be maximising its global growth potential.

A third contextual analysis applies to both the corporate and operational levels. This is business exposure. The specific issues and assets might vary between the corporate and operational levels but the broader concept of exposure, in terms of people, reputation and performance is similar to both. This element of analysis is necessary because in the absence of an understanding of what it is *at risk*, risk analysis is purely academic and it is difficult to draw actionable insights.

RISK TOLERANCE DEFINITION

Imagine that the company sees a strong opportunity in a country with record of instability and weak governance. If the venture was in Europe or North America, it would be an easy decision, but given the country's reputation it is more complex. Without an up-front understanding of its own tolerance for risk, the firm could weigh the pros and cons endlessly. With a clear benchmark of its appetite for risk, the decision is simplified at least up to the point of opting whether to invest more resources in investigating the opportunity in detail. The aim of risk tolerance definition is to set this benchmark.

The basic question is, 'Where do we draw the line in terms of political risk?' To address this, a company needs to integrate information about itself and its industry. For example, where are its competitors operating, and where is the market growing? What is our culture in relation to risk? How well could we absorb the liabilities if serious political risk was incurred? Finally, how equipped are we to manage political risk? Each of these factors can be rated to form an initial indication of the firm's tolerance, as Figure 4.1 illustrates.

The sum of scores for indication of risk tolerance is divided by the total number of factors to yield an average score. For example, if each factor favoured risk-taking, then the total would be 12, which divided by four yields an average score of three, 'favours risk-taking'.

The final score can then be aligned to countries or regions in high, medium and low risk brackets (perhaps as provided by country risk rating agencies) where there is a reasonably strong market for the firm's products or services. For example, for typical large IT services firms the low-risk end might be represented by North America and Western Europe, the middle bracket represented by Central Europe, and the risky bracket by the Middle East and India. For the extractives sector the whole spectrum would reach from North America to some of the most volatile countries in the world, such as Sudan or the Democratic Republic of Congo.

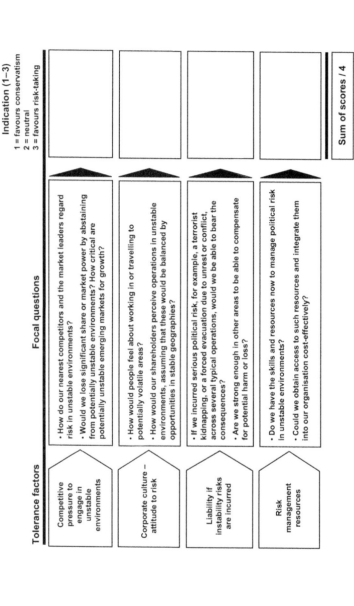

Tolerance factors

Focal questions

Indication (1–3)
1 = favours conservatism
2 = neutral
3 = favours risk-taking

Competitive pressure to engage in unstable environments

- How do our nearest competitors and the market leaders regard risk in unstable environments?
- Would we lose significant share or market power by abstaining from potentially unstable environments? How critical are potentially unstable emerging markets for growth?

Corporate culture – attitude to risk

- How would people feel about working in or travelling to potentially volatile areas?
- How would our shareholders perceive operations in unstable environments, assuming that these would be balanced by opportunities in stable geographies?

Liability if instability risks are incurred

- If we incurred serious political risk, for example, a terrorist kidnapping, or a forced evacuation due to unrest or conflict, across several typical operations, would we be able to bear the consequences?
- Are we strong enough in other areas to be able to compensate for potential harm or loss?

Risk management resources

- Do we have the skills and resources now to manage political risk in unstable environments?
- Could we obtain access to such resources and integrate them into our organisation cost-effectively?

Sum of scores / 4

Figure 4.1 Risk tolerance definition model

If the firm aligns its risk tolerance rating to the appropriate representative region, it will then know where its 'red line' is in terms of operating environments. For example, if an IT services firm finds a strong opportunity in West Africa, which would be at the far end of its high-risk bracket, and its risk tolerance was only 2 – neutral, then it could start with the premise that the opportunity lies beyond its appetite for risk.

Another benefit of this exercise is that it provides some indication not just of current risk tolerance, but of how risk tolerant a company should be if it seeks to be a serious contender in emerging markets. If everybody else has a neutral tolerance, for example, then one could see a clear benefit in developing a risk-taking attitude and capability in order to break free of the pack and pursue opportunities where others prefer not to go. There might be no point in this strategy if the market in high-risk regions is small or negligible, but if there is considerable unmet demand in such regions then this could be a reasonable conclusion from this exercise.

GLOBAL POLITICAL RISK PORTFOLIO ASSESSMENT

The global political risk portfolio assessment seeks to discern the degree of overall political risk facing the company across all of its operations. Too much risk indicates that exposure might need to be adjusted in the future to make the overall business more sustainable. Too little risk could indicate opportunities to take more chances in terms of global spread, on the basis that risk often does lead to reward in terms of access to new markets, cheaper labour and materials, and more efficient supply routes.

There are three steps to the portfolio assessment:

1. Define the strategic relevance of each of the company's international operations.

2. Discern the relative level of political risk in each operating location.

3. Map the results to elucidate the global risk portfolio.

The strategic relevance of an operation is generally a factor of the operation's commercial benefits in terms of global growth and competitive advantage; the assets exposed in the operation (people, reputation, physical and financial assets and so on); and the importance of the operation to the achievement of the firm's strategic aspirations. These can be aggregated to yield a strategic relevance score for each location.

The relative level of political risk in a location can be discerned by placing it on scale ranging from low to high risk, with well-known benchmark countries representing each bracket. The end-points of the scale should be representative of the firm's industry more broadly, that is, the least and highest risk locations where industry growth leaders have significant operations. If the scale only includes the company's own operating locations, then it fails to reveal opportunities to adjust the portfolio beyond the firm's current parameters. Again, a country's relative risk rating could be drawn from country rating service providers, with the caveat that any model used should integrate the spectrum of instability, conflict and weak governance, and not just a country's financial standing.

Each operation is then positioned on a matrix, with one axis being political risk in the location, and the other the operation's strategic relevance. This reveals the global political risk portfolio. Two hypothetical outcomes for firms in the same industry are illustrated in Figure 4.2 below.

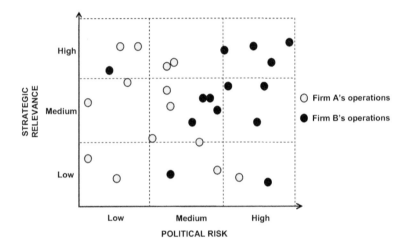

Figure 4.2   Illustrative global political risk portfolios

In this case, two of Firm A's operations define the least risky end of the political risk scale in this industry, while one of Firm B's operations defines the highest risk end. The rest of the operations fall somewhere in between. Clearly Firm B is taking more chances, and is becoming overstretched and vulnerable to strategic disruption arising from political risk. Perhaps it needs to seek more opportunities in less risky places to decrease its vulnerability. Firm A, on the other hand, is playing it safe, perhaps too safe. It could be missing out on the higher rewards that often come with playing in higher risk environments.

How the portfolio is interpreted will of course depend to an extent on the current corporate strategy. Perhaps A was an early leader in well established markets and prefers to entrench there to hold its position, while B might be a latecomer and has decided to take more risks in order to catch up. Regardless, without a picture of the risk portfolio, a firm will not fully understand whether or not it actually has managed to implement its global risk strategy, and knowing the risk portfolio can indeed be the starting point in deciding what that strategy should be.

BUSINESS EXPOSURE

Again this analysis varies between the corporate and operational levels, but it is similar in concept. The principal difference is in nuance. The corporate level is concerned with all business operations and all locations, therefore an assessment of exposure is necessarily abstract. The operational level is concerned about a specific initiative in one location, hence exposure can be defined more sharply. In the last chapter we defined the principal assets exposed to political risk. Here we will look instead at how to assess the degree of exposure in a firm or operation's specific context.

People   The company as a whole will have a certain percentage of its personnel working overseas in emerging markets. The greater this percentage is, the higher its exposure to political risk in terms of people. Within this set, a certain percentage will be expatriates, including dependents. Expats face higher risk than national staff through their unfamiliarity with their operating environment, incur greater duty of care obligation since they are in a new location at the company's behest, and therefore represent higher exposure. Therefore in general terms a firm's personnel exposure to political risk is primarily a factor of the percentage of its workforce who are expats working in potentially unstable developing countries.

At the operational level the equation is similar. While all people are important assets, again the proportion of expats drives personnel exposure, for the reasons mentioned above. One difference at the operational level is that duty of care to national personnel will be regulated by the laws of the host country, therefore the degree of liability for national staff can vary considerably between operations.

Reputation   At the corporate level, reputational exposure is defined by three factors. One is the firm's past performance in terms of corporate citizenship and governance. The weaker this is, the more exposed the firm is to the attention of critics and to negative characterisation.

Another factor is the general reputation of the sector the firm is in. Direction and degree of criticism vary depending on sector. For example, pharmaceutical firms have been criticised by governments and NGOs for overpricing, monopoly practices involving widely needed drugs, and sometimes unethical testing. Likewise extractive firms have been associated with environmental decay, collusion with abusive regimes in their operating locations, and for unnecessarily prolonging global reliance on fossil fuels. However 'clean' the firm's track record, its reputation will inevitably be exposed to critiques aimed at its wider sector.

Finally, the political symbolism of the firm is a factor. It will often be associated with the foreign policy of its home government. As well, however objective the firm's selection of overseas operations might be in practice, any perceived preference for work in countries which could be regarded as rivals of others, or as negative influences on regional or global stability, can also incur ideologically motivated criticism.

At the operational level, a project will bring the corporate 'baggage' with them in terms of all of the above, but these will be magnified or reinterpreted by the specific operating environment. The company's past track record in a country can be a major element of reputational scrutiny, regardless of how well a firm has performed globally. The firm's sector can have sharper implications, depending on the host country's experience with other foreign firms in the same sector. The political symbolism of the firm running the project will obviously be a factor in local ideologically inspired scrutiny. For example, a US firm operating in Guatemala can expect considerably more attention than an Italian firm doing broadly the same kind of work. Likewise, if the project is being run by a firm with a track record of work in a rival country, it would likely incur higher scrutiny.

Performance   In assessing exposure in terms of performance at the corporate level, a company needs to define its critical success factors in international operations generally. These then become the critical assets exposed to political risk. For example, an automobile manufacturer with an extended global supply chain and assembly plants in diverse locations will rely on: business continuity of its suppliers and its own plants; open and dependable supply routes for shipping parts and products; dependable labour sources; host government respect for foreign property rights; stable currency regimes, and so on. It is likely that critical global performance assets will be very similar for firms in the same sector, and by the same token vary considerably across sectors.

At the operational level critical performance assets are more nuanced. For example, if a firm is building a new airport terminal in North Africa, it will rely on all of the generic corporate-level performance assets, but also: dependable functioning of the city's port for the import of heavy equipment; reliable traffic infrastructure between the port and the airport; smooth relations with the local union and labour authorities; timely granting of import and building licences, and so on. The control element of performance is also more important, and exposure in this sense can be linked to the type of contract and how it was awarded (the more open the process, the more control a foreign firm will have); foreign investment regulations governing national stakes or ownership, local content and currency repatriation; and the past performance of local partners and the state in terms of contract fulfilment and compliance with commercial agreements.

In a sense, performance-related assets are the assumptions that a company makes about its commercial success. When operating in volatile regions, these assumptions can break down in the face of political risk, and hence they represent political risk exposure.

A full list or detailed analysis of all possible ways that a business or operation is exposed to political risk is probably unfeasible and certainly unnecessary. It is sufficient to develop a clear understanding of our key assets exposed when operating in potentially unstable environments. By undertaking this exercise we are already generating hypotheses about relevant types of risk, and are primed with the background we need to conduct an actionable risk assessment.

RISK ANALYSIS

Armed with the context with which to interpret risk, we now directly identify risks and assess priority issues. The aim is not to identify every possible way that the political environment might affect us. A certain amount of business planning takes into account that things go wrong, and contingencies are a normal part of any strategy. We will instead focus on deriving significant risks, and from these we will define an even smaller priority set which requires explicit mitigation planning, as discussed in the following chapter.

The process of political risk analysis is common to both the corporate and operational levels, and has three stages, as outlined in Figure 4.3 below.

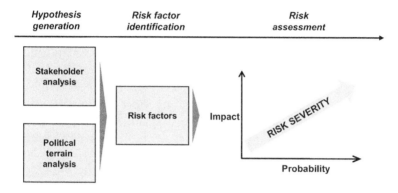

Figure 4.3   Political risk analysis process

Hypothesis generation examines how we might affect political interests through our activities. Those affected will develop an attitude towards the business, either friendly or hostile, and hostile interests will probably react to us in some way. Their potential reactions could harm us, and therefore become risk factors that we need consider.

This phase also examines the exogenous political terrain, that is, what is happening in the given political environment (global or local) irrespective of our presence or activities. Some trends and conditions would be harmful if we were exposed to them, and these too become risk factors.

Next we assess the potential effect of risk factors on our key exposed assets. Where an asset could suffer harm, the intersection of the risk factor and exposed asset then becomes an actual risk. Each risk is then assessed in terms of the impact on us if it did occur, and the probability of its occurrence. Risks are then mapped to define priorities. The priorities become the focus of risk management initiatives.

The principal difference between the corporate and operational levels in this process is again the level of abstraction. At the corporate, global level we are dealing with global interests and issues, and this level is necessarily more abstract than the operational one, which focuses on a specific initiative in one location. The logic, however, is the same. We will examine each step, highlighting key distinctions between the two management levels as they arise.

HYPOTHESIS GENERATION

Stakeholder Analysis   The stakeholder analysis process is as follows:

1. Identify types of political actors who *could* have an interest in the firm's behaviour, and influence over the firm.

2. Identify specific actors within each broad type.

3. Through research, assess the favourability and influence of each stakeholder, and group them according to similar levels of favour/disfavour and influence.

4. Map stakeholders on a matrix from which actionable conclusions can be easily drawn.

Defining broad types of stakeholders can rely on past learning in overseas operations, and general knowledge about the experience of other firms in similar sectors and political environments. At both the corporate and operational levels, stakeholder types generally include, but are not limited to:

- political leadership,

- non-violent political opposition groups,

- regulators, both national and transnational (for example, US Department of Commerce or the World Trade Organisation [WTO]),

- transnational organisations which set non-binding but still influential ethical business standards (for example, the UN or OECD),

- civil society, in particular as it represented through NGOs and labour unions, and the media, and

- violent opposition or extremist groups.

The principal difference between stakeholders relevant to the corporate and operational levels is not so much in type, but in scope of influence or activity, that is, global or local. For each of the above categories we can find examples which have global influence, and those with more constrained reach. This even applies to national governments. All are mainly concerned with domestic affairs, but some are very active internationally.

There is also a middle ground between global and local actors, for example, global NGOs or transnational organisations with a global remit but with initiatives running in numerous specific countries. The corporate concern would be those actors with global reach and remit, and the operational level would focus more on actors with especially strong influence in their specific operating environment, whether these are global actors or, more often, national or local ones.

After defining types of actors, we can search for specific ones with particular relevance to our own business interests, then assess their potential attitude towards our activities, and their potential influence over us. The model shown in Figure 4.4 provides a guideline for this process.

Notice that we also include 'How could they support us?' under potential influence. When we come to consider risk management, one of our options would be to cultivate relationships with favourable stakeholders in order to counter the influence of unfavourable ones, or to support us in any other appropriate way. For example, a local NGO might start with a lukewarm attitude towards our project, but then when engaged in the firm's corporate social responsibility activities its attitude could improve and it could become a valuable partner in helping us to gain acceptance in the wider host community. Our focus right now is on risk, but this exercise simultaneously finds potential risk mitigation options which later become relevant.

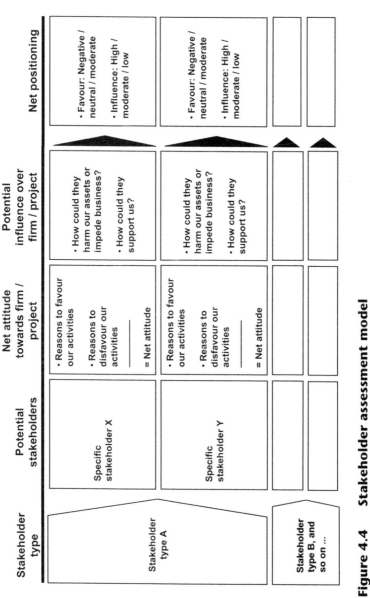

Stakeholder type	Potential stakeholders	Net attitude towards firm / project	Potential influence over firm / project	Net positioning
Stakeholder type A	Specific stakeholder X	• Reasons to favour our activities • Reasons to disfavour our activities _____ = Net attitude	• How could they harm our assets or impede business? • How could they support us?	• Favour: Negative / neutral / moderate • Influence: High / moderate / low
	Specific stakeholder Y	• Reasons to favour our activities • Reasons to disfavour our activities _____ = Net attitude	• How could they harm our assets or impede business? • How could they support us?	• Favour: Negative / neutral / moderate • Influence: High / moderate / low
Stakeholder type B, and so on …				

Figure 4.4   Stakeholder assessment model

At this point, stakeholders can be mapped according to the assessment, as illustrated below in Figure 4.5 (this is somewhat simplified – in practice there would likely be more stakeholders).

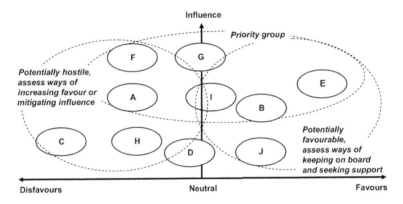

Figure 4.5   Stakeholder map

We now have our priority stakeholders, and we have an indication of how they could react to us (that is, specific types of influence driven by attitude). The potential negative reactions become risk factors. In addition, we have another piece of intelligence stored away for risk management planning: potentially supportive stakeholders.

Political Terrain Analysis   To reiterate, we not only need to understand our potential effect on political interests and how that generates risks, but we need to know what is happening in our operating environment irrespective of our presence. Imagine flying over a country and parachuting out. Even before you hit the ground, there will be a lot going on, and the people and companies already there will be experiencing the effects of a unique set of political trends and conditions.

Once you land, you might have an impact on the situation, but you will also be subjected to the same risks as anyone else. We need to understand these exogenous risks.

A natural starting point is a scan of relevant trends within each of the principal sources, or drivers, of risk: instability; weak governance; and conflict (as defined in the last chapter). We know from the previous two chapters what kinds of risk are associated with a heightening of each source of risk. If we understand the pace and direction of the evolution of each source, then we can develop hypotheses about relevant risk factors at the appropriate level of analysis, global or operational.

There are differences between the corporate and operational levels in this exercise, not in the type of trends under the microscope, but in the level of abstraction. At the corporate level we are seeking an understanding of risk factors relevant to our operations in emerging markets generally, and especially in regions where we have considerable interests. At this level, what we are really doing is aggregating what happens across a range of countries, to try to get an overview of global and regional issues. At the operational level, we are dealing with a single country or sub-part thereof, and therefore we can reasonably hope to obtain a much more nuanced and detailed level of understanding. That being said, the types of trends are the same. The corporate level simply aggregates country-specific information at a higher level of abstraction.

Chapters 2 and 3 have already highlighted some relevant trends and risks that derive from them, but we can suggest a few observable trend indicators here which are commonly applied in analyses of the exogenous political terrain, as follows.

INSTABILITY – INCREASING/SAME/DECREASING: CONSIDER

- Democratisation, legal political opposition and political institutionalisation, or lack thereof.

- Presence/persistence of interim governments.

- Incidence and intensity of civil unrest, strikes and violent protest.

- Military/security intervention in politics (legacy of coups d'état, shadow governments [the latter is often hard to discern but is indicative of significant splits and dysfunction of the 'official' regime]).

- Social discontent with the pace of economic development and improvements in the standard of living (manifesting through protest or labour action, and political declarations from civil interest groups and NGOs).

- Routine and harsh repression (as tracked by human rights groups and donor governments).

WEAK GOVERNANCE – INCREASING/SAME/DECREASING: CONSIDER

- Dominance and prevalence of key personalities in politics.

- Abrupt changes in policy and law with lack of regard for representative or judicial institutions.

- Eccentric patterns of state repression.

- Regular intervention of key regime figures in deals or decisions over which they have no 'official' remit.

- Heavy-handed and opaque control of government revenues.

- Corruption, both at the high and low ends of officialdom.

- Evidence of collusion between the regime and criminal interests.

CONFLICT – INCREASING/SAME/DECREASING: CONSIDER

- Persistent friction between two or more sides and an inability to reach consensus, as manifesting in political vitriol.

- A legacy of routine or regular armed clashes between two or more sides, each with either very divergent political visions, territorial aspirations or economic interests.

- The persistent presence of sub-national political groups with ready access to arms, fighters and command and control infrastructure, whether or not combat is occurring.

- Unresolved major tensions between different ethnic, communal or ideological groups.

- Regular terrorist attacks in terms of covertly implemented bombings and raids on ideologically symbolic targets.

- A state of high tension or declared war with another/other countries.

Not all of these will be relevant or discernable to a specific international company, but some in each category will be. After addressing these questions of our relevant operating environment(s), we should be in a reasonably strong position to identify relevant risk factors.

There is another, less rigorous but still useful exercise towards discerning exogenous risk. This is simply the observation of what has happened with our own and similar firms in the recent past. From such an analysis, we can gain not just an understanding of indications of potential risk, but also of actual risk that we might face. Relevant questions, at both the global and operational levels, could include:

- What has happened to other, similar firms operating in the same kinds of environment in the past? What risks did they encounter?

- As an experienced manager on the ground, what did you see, what happened, how would you deconstruct this to arrive at an idea of what risk was incurred?

- Given your best intelligence, what are you concerned about, and why?

Information from experienced sources might be highly anecdotal or the causes of manifested risk could be badly misinterpreted. Nonetheless, given its ground-level proximity, and with sufficient corroboration, it forms a useful part of the broader analysis.

After both exercises (trend analysis and first-hand insights) we have an understanding of the kinds of risks we might face as a result of the environments we are now or are moving into. These, in addition to the risks arising from our stakeholder interaction, are taken forward as risk factors.

RISK ASSESSMENT

From the contextual analysis of our exposure, and from the risk factors identified through stakeholder analysis and our look at the relevant political terrain, we can match the assets that we expose to risk factors to derive our actual risks, and then derive priorities among these.

There are four steps to this process:

1. Assess our exposure against risk factors to decide which factors could really affect our assets.

2. Assess the potential impact of a risk if it occurred, independently of a risk's probability of occurrence.

3. Assess the probability of a risk occurring, independently of its potential impact.

4. Map the results to derive priority risks.

The first step is a matter of looking at how any given risk factor might really affect us. For example, if a military coup occurred, would we be significantly affected? If we were an exporter of consumer goods with flexible contractual terms, then we could reasonably regard this risk as 'latent' – that is, not really relevant to us, for now. If on the other hand we were a mining or construction company with significant assets, including people, on the ground in the middle of fulfilling a multi-year contract, it would be an actual risk, that is, something that could directly affect our assets now or in the near future.

In looking at the impact of a risk, the immediate effects of a manifested risk will matter, but to understand the full impact we also need to look at a risk's reverberations. If, for example, a foreign construction company is operating on a state contract in a country which is facing an imminent military coup, the immediate effects might include: a gap in law enforcement performance as security forces try to decide whom they are working for, and therefore a gap in security; closure of borders and main transport routes as the new regime tries to prevent upsets to its fragile position, and therefore a gap in business continuity; and hazards to national personnel as the new regime conducts general round-ups of anyone remotely antithetical to its takeover. But this is not the whole story. Reverberations could include: reputational fallout for the firm for its affiliation with a military junta; sanctions against the new regime which severely constrain the import of necessary materials; and the renegotiation of the contract which was established with the old and now illegal government.

In assessing impact, it is useful to apply a diagrammatic model which we loosely call an 'impact timeline' as illustrated in Figure 4.6 below.

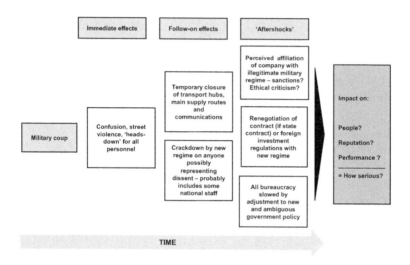

Figure 4.6   Impact timeline for coup d'état

We can now assess the full impact of the risk. How serious is it for us if it happens? What is the net effect on our combined exposed assets? Some benchmarks using commonly understood meanings can facilitate this assessment. For example, if we select a three point scale we might have: 1 as 'worrying'; 2 as 'harmful'; and 3 as 'serious'. In the example of a construction company operating in volatile environments, a 'worrying' impact might be persistent and disconcerting demands for bribes from state clients and officials, and 'serious' could be the long-term cessation or premature closure of the operation, or the non-accidental loss of life. Some impacts might fall between the benchmarks, and a final subjective adjustment is often useful.

Probability, the likelihood of a risk manifesting, is derived from past trends in terms of frequency or prevalence in the operating environment(s), and current trends which might affect near-term future frequency or prevalence. We can use a basic rating system with the same number of benchmarks as in our assessment of impact, in this case 1 to 3. Again we can suggest some common sense benchmarks, with 1 as 'unlikely', 2 as 'possible', and 3 as 'likely'. These should be backed up by numerical probabilities to ensure alignment in terms of interpretation, for example: 1 is 10–30 per cent, 2 is 31–55 per cent, 3 is 56–100 per cent (Note that in risk management we tend to err on the side of caution: this illustrative scale is skewed to favour an expectation of risks manifesting). If a risk is less probable than ten percent, it is probably a peripheral risk worth noting as such but not worth inclusion in the full analytical process. Again, a final subjective adjustment will be useful to distinguish specific risks.

Having assessed probability and impact, we can map the results to discern priority risks. This conclusive step is illustrated at a hypothetical level in Figure 4.7; it is simpler than most real-world results, but still indicative of the logic. Note that although this example applies to the project level, most of the risk factors here would also apply to the global level, although that is by no means always the case in practice.

We should keep an eye on all of the risks on the map, but the priorities would rightfully be the main focus of risk management planning.

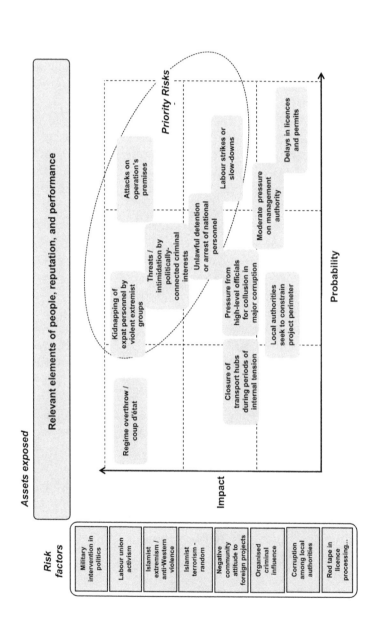

Figure 4.7   Risk prioritisation matrix

SCENARIO ANALYSIS

Risk analysis reveals priority current and near-term issues, but the whole political environment might shift within our operating horizon. Not every risk would change as a result, but we still need to be aware of long-term shifts to be able to plan our own gradual adaptation to an evolving situation. The future is uncertain, and scenario analysis is a tool which enables us to at least see what *could* happen, and to identify possible future states of most relevance to our interests.

There are a variety of methods in scenario analysis, ranging from common-sense thumbnail sketches of future states, to mathematical approaches. The more detailed or technical the approach, the more precise the results, but not necessarily the more accurate – even the most sophisticated models are ultimately based on judgement. One drawback of complex methods is that those using the results, that is, those involved in risk management planning, might not be comfortable with how conclusions were derived, or how to really interpret them.

We therefore suggest an approach here which balances complexity and intuitive interpretation. It is derived from an intelligence model called 'competing hypotheses', in which several hypotheses of the future state are posited, and then a story is mapped to fulfil each. The plausibility of each hypothesis can then be assessed based on the probability that specific variables would change as required to make it come true, and on the strength of the linkages between the variables.

There are six steps to this process:

1. Define the hypotheses.

2. Identify relevant variables (our risk factors taken from the risk analysis) and the drivers that influence them.

3. Consider causal linkages between all variables.

4. Define stories for each hypothesis (these stories are in effect the scenarios).

5. Assess the plausibility of each scenario.

6. Define warnings and indicators for each scenario.

An overview of the model is depicted in Figure 4.8. The variables selected are hypothetical; the important point to note is the more abstract, broader character of the change drivers – each driver, while not an immediate issue for us, could affect several risk factors.

We use four hypotheses in this approach. Because we are dealing with uncertain future states, it is useful not to have a middle ground, since this assumes no change from the current state and people tend to gravitate towards what they know; in fact given a three- to five-year projection (reasonable in political risk) there will almost inevitably be some change. As risk managers, we will be most interested in the negative outcomes, but we still need to focus on a range of potential outcomes or we risk fixating on only the negative, and likely over-hyping it.

The relevant variables begin with our risk factors, as identified previously. Then for each one we look one or two steps back,

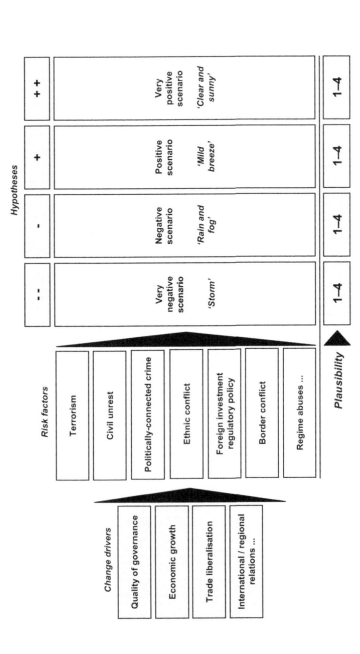

Figure 4.8   Scenario analysis overview

posing the question, 'What makes this factor more or less intense or prevalent?' Thereby we identify our drivers. We will likely come up with a range of drivers, some of which will apply to several risk factors. It is useful to group drivers under aggregate headings in order to simplify the analysis. For example, we might discern democratisation, political institutionalisation, changes in adherence to the rule of law, and compliance with ethical and transparent standards of governance as drivers, but they fit well into the broader heading of 'governance'.

In order to develop the scenarios, we need to understand how the different variables affect each other. This applies not just to the relationship between drivers and risk factors, but also between different risk factors. Terrorism, for example, can increase a regime's propensity towards abuse as they crack down on civil society to try to fight it. Similarly, a border conflict with a neighbouring state with a dominant ethnic group which is a minority in the host country can increase ethnic tensions.

A useful way to get to grips with linkages is to visually map the 'risk system', or the inter-linkages between the variables. We illustrate this mapping in Figure 4.9, using only a few of the variables from the above overview.

Notice that linkages can occur between drivers, between drivers and risk factors, and between different risk factors. All levels need to be considered. When we write a scenario, much of the 'plot' will be in the form of 'as A increases, B will become less acute, leading to an attenuation of C ... and so on'. Linkages are key in developing a robust plot.

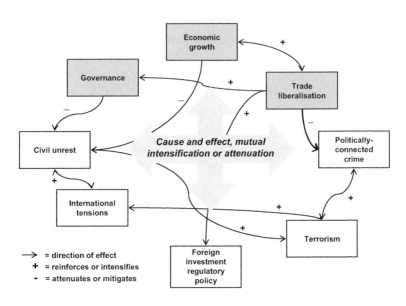

Figure 4.9   Risk system map

We now create a scenario for each hypothesis. We are effectively addressing the question, 'If things were to go this way, what would have to happen?' We would usually start with the behaviour of the drivers, or the macro-trends, and work our way down to risk factors, and ultimately to the risks to our operation. Linkages would be explained along the way, and any given change in one factor would be supported by, or affect, other trends in the system. A typical scenario can be quite long and complex, but we should aim for a coherent summary version of about two pages for the sake of clarity and management attention.

When developing scenarios, we might sense that a certain hypothesis is unlikely and feel tentative or even absurd trying to explain how it might come about. We need to be creative and not afraid to introduce unlikely events or changes into the story. The whole point, after all, is to avoid surprises, and in any case we will be assessing plausibility independently.

Next we assess the plausibility of each scenario. We use 'plausibility' because it is more appropriate to the assessment of complex storylines than 'probability', which lends itself better to the treatment of discrete risks. Plausibility is based on our sense of the probability of specific key trigger events or trends in a scenario actually occurring, consistency with past trends, and the strength of the causal linkages that we have posited to fulfil a given hypothesis. Plausibility can be rated using a basic system, with, for example, 1 as 'highly doubtful', 2 as 'somewhat dubious', 3 as 'believable', and 4 as 'quite credible'. The exact labels are not really important as long as they convey the appropriate meaning among a shared readership.

From a risk management perspective, the intersection of negativity and plausibility defines the priority scenarios, although given the implications of the worst one, we need to keep an eye on that no matter how dubious. The positive scenarios are useful counterbalances to our professional inclination towards the negative, and can also help our colleagues in strategy and marketing to take advantage of improving situations through more aggressive commercial planning.

The final step of the analysis is to enable planners to foresee the emergence of priority scenarios through the development of warnings and indicators, that is, observable, detectable trends or events that forewarn of the future evolving in the direction of a priority scenario.

Observable, detectable trends or events are those which are usually tracked by the media, commercial intelligence providers or government agencies who make a degree of relevant information available to the public. In some cases we might have specialised sources with unique access to a given factor, such as a lawyer actively involved in international trade negotiations or a counter-terrorist security expert with an insider's perspective on the Global War on Terror, but these will be the exceptions, so selecting warnings and indicators on the basis of open source access is advisable.

We can define several degrees of emergence of a scenario, such as 'latent', 'active' (that is, there is a degree of change towards emergence), and 'emerging' (that is, the scenario or a variant thereof appears to be unfolding). Each degree would be signified by a specific set of trends and events. For a negative scenario, for example, the 'active' degree might be indicated by slower-than-expected economic growth recovery, high unemployment, trade disputes, the frequency and intensity of ethnic clashes, and so on.

As with risk analysis, in scenario analysis the principal distinction between the corporate/global and operational levels is the degree of abstraction. Global scenarios will examine macro-trends with implications across a range of regions and for international investment in the relevant sector generally. Operational scenarios will focus more on trends relevant to the sustainability of a project in one country or part thereof. There might be some cross-over between the variables used, but the two levels are distinct. The trick at the global level is to constrain the focus to globally relevant variables, and not to get bogged down in trying to build up a big picture on the basis of a diversity of smaller, localised ones. If anything, global scenarios can be even more concise, since they focus on top-level trends and do not have to consider a high degree of nuance.

SUMMARY

We began with three analyses that enable us to interpret risk in our context. At the corporate level, we have systematically defined our tolerance for risk, and we know the overall level of risk across our global portfolio of operations. Both of these help us to understand when we are exceeding our tolerance for political risk, and to identify opportunities to take on more risk. We also defined our risk exposure, so that we know what political risks are relevant to us. Next we conducted the risk analysis, to derive the risks that we need to focus on most. Finally, we attained an understanding of how the whole political environment might shift over time, and how different emerging futures could affect us. At this point we have the intelligence we need for actionable risk management planning, the subject of the next chapter.

NOTE ON ANALYTICAL TRAPS

A chapter on analysis is not complete without raising some of the common failings that people have when undertaking estimative assessment. There is much useful commentary on this issue so we can afford to be brief. In short, estimates are always subject to our own biases, and to our propensity to fill in the gaps with preconceptions and popularly accepted 'myths'. We tend to latch onto what we know or believe, and use this certainty, however inapplicable to the issues we are examining, as screens to shape our interpretation of new information. We also try to tailor assessments for what we think our audience wants to hear or what they expect. The end result can be misleading or ineffectual assessments.

Analytical traps are especially relevant in political risk assessments. First, we all have relatively strong ideological biases, and in assessing a political environment these often form our normative lens in terms of the interpretation of negative and positive trends. Second, unlike other areas of business, such as marketing or process optimisation, little in political risk is easily measurable in terms of numbers; even when numerical models are used they derive more from informed judgement than by counting observable units. Thus the subjective factor is greater, and interpretation becomes more art than science.

Logical and robust analytical frameworks, and structured questioning which forces us to stretch our comfort zones can help to get beyond our own psychological constraints. However, we need to actively seek alternative points of view and be ready to challenge our own preconceptions. Part of a strong analytical process is the application of a devil's advocate system, whereby another team or analyst examines the same facts on hand and tries to shape them differently to see if they might actually point to different conclusions. This is not always feasible in terms of time and resources, but the reader, either already or perhaps one day a user of political risk intelligence, should be aware of the traps that analysts can fall into, and be ready to challenge conclusions if they feel that there are some inexplicable logical leaps between facts and interpretation.

A good source for further reading on this issue is Richard J. Heuer, *Psychology of Intelligence Analysis* (Center for the Study of Intelligence, Central Intelligence Agency, 1999). This and other texts on the subject are useful for analysts and intelligence consumers alike.

(5) Political Risk Management

OVERVIEW

We understand the priority political risk issues in the areas relevant to our organisation and interests. How do we act on this intelligence to mitigate risk? That is the subject of this chapter.

Political risk management, as we alluded to in Chapter 1, is an elusive concept in the sense that it is not an established management function and cross-cuts existing capabilities. Nonetheless, it needs form and function to enable coherent responses to risk. In this chapter, we will attempt to provide insights on the wider concept of political risk management, how coherence can be achieved, and specific options and measures.

This chapter will examine:

- The concept of political risk management.

- The linkage between intelligence and action.

- Political risk management measures.

- Organisational structures to enable coherent and holistic political risk management.

- The evaluation of political risk management performance.

- The concept of a political risk management strategy.

The Appendix, 'The Political Risk Consulting Landscape' forms a useful adjunct to organisational structures, the fourth point above.

POLITICAL RISK MANAGEMENT CONCEPT

Before addressing the nuts and bolts of political risk management, it is useful to have a top-level understanding of what this function is trying to achieve. There are two useful notions: resilience; and political risk management as an enabler of global strategy.

RESILIENCE

The term 'political risk management' has been regarded as knowing the bad things that could happen to us in developing countries and preparing ourselves for damage limitation. However, this trouble-shooting perspective limits us to reactivity and an 'us and them' dichotomy which can indeed incur conflictual relationships through our perceived anxiety about engaging with host communities and the global environment. Rather, we can regard political risk management as enabling the fulfilment of objectives in even high-risk political environments. From this we arrive at the idea of resilience.

Resilience means being able to flex without breaking. Imagine a bamboo plant in a tropical forest. It reaches high up to obtain sunlight, but the narrow diameter of each strand means that it does not impede other plants from getting light, and thereby minimises conflict. Bamboo has a hard shell, protecting a soft inner core against predators, friction with other plants and the wind and rain. It flexes at extreme angles to avoid threats and to accommodate others' interests, but is capable of bouncing back when it has the space. It has tenacious roots and is hard to eradicate.

Resilience, as characterised above, is a useful conceptualisation of the aim of political risk management, which can be regarded as thoughtfully positioned strands of high-tensile steel in the wider edifice of an organisation operating in volatile environments.

STRATEGIC ENABLEMENT

Competition for markets, labour and supplies has become intense with globalisation. A firm capable of extending beyond its comfort zones is better positioned to achieve its global objectives than many competitors. In the global context, political risk management is a strategic enabler. Those who are not skilled in this regard are justifiably hesitant to approach the peripheries of their established business terrain, while others can plant roots in new territories as beachheads for growth and access to lower cost inputs. They can even make their competency in political risk management a barrier to entry for their competitors, albeit likely a temporary one.

Imagine, for example, that we are an international retail grocery group. After a global market scan we identify a vibrant and unfulfilled grocery market in West Africa, in terms of demand for international products and the convenience of one-stop shopping and consistent customer service. Really gaining traction there would mean branded stores with consistent customer service and a steady international supply chain, and these would require exposing ourselves directly to the regional and local political environments.

We still, of course, need to compete in familiar geographies. We can still differentiate through brand, pricing, channels and product offerings. But these are options for any of our current competitors, and every new idea implemented on mutually familiar terrain soon becomes a new battleground. Gains are incremental and short-lived.

The typical international retailer, that is, a competitor, sees neighbourhoods, cities/towns and countries in areas of close cultural or geo-proximity to its home market as its competitive terrain. If an area is roughly similar to its home turf, then adaptation is possible. Going beyond this exceeds the *risk tolerance* of many of our competitors. There could be an opportunity to put this conservatism to our advantage if we really were able to handle more risk than they could.

What if we can add West Africa to our market portfolio? It is not the most savoury environment for companies used to Europe and North America: there is very considerable political risk. But other foreign companies in different sectors have done well there. Why not us? Imagine that after considerable research and learning through small-scale trial and error we eventually open several outlets in the region, perhaps in the capitols of Nigeria, Ivory Coast and Cameroon to start. These pilots do reasonably well and expand into more significant operations.

Most other competitors are still fixated on traditional markets and have yet not invested the time and resources to learn how to operate in West Africa or similar terrain. But a few especially aggressive competitors do try to catch our lead. Several fail badly because of encounters with political risk in the environment – they thought that because one of their peers did it, so could they. They did not realise how much time and attention we initially paid to learning and navigating political risk in the region. With fingers burnt they retreat to safer terrain. Some will succeed, but by then we will be well ahead on the emerging market learning curve.

Thus we have gained a new growth opportunity which for a while at least eludes our main competitors, and allows us not only to augment revenue, but to learn from this experience to make headway in comparable territories and in our evolution as a globally capable firm.

In this scenario, political risk management is a key element. Without it, the hypothetical European firm would in many ways be walking into a minefield and if implementation outpaced understanding, it could have faced a major strategic disruption. As it was, with learning and experimentation it succeeded in developing a solid new component of its growth portfolio.

If we know that we can manage ourselves in potentially volatile terrain, then our risk tolerance justifiably increases beyond that of our competitors, and we can seek opportunities where they would not dare to follow, at least not until we show them how, by which time we have a significant lead. In some industries, political risk management could be a new tool of growth and actually cause some strategic disruption in the industry. In others, such as the extractives sector, it is already a baseline success factor, and the advantage lies with those who do it better rather than with those who do it at all.

The main point to derive from the concepts of resilience and strategic enablement is that political risk management is not just about damage limitation. The aim is to succeed in spite of the risks, and to stretch our limitations to become a capable global player.

INTELLIGENCE TO ACTION

After a dip into the conceptual side, we can return to the routine aspects of political risk management with affirmation of its relevance. To begin with, we undertook risk analysis for a good reason: we sensed that our company is relying more and more heavily on emerging market opportunities as part of its growth strategy; second, several of our operations are in places where the political 'rules of the game' are ill-defined yet represent a major variable in our success. We sought to learn more about the political environment, and now we need to transform this learning, or intelligence, into action. This process is illustrated in Figure 5.1.

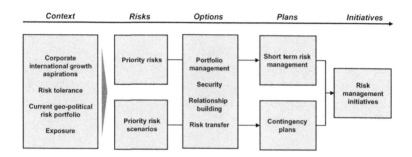

Figure 5.1   Intelligence to action

We start with something that was not explicitly addressed here, corporate ambitions: targets that would be set in the context of capabilities, competition and demand at a global level, that is, why we are bothering with potentially volatile environments in the first place. We also take into account our risk tolerance and global spread, and our global or operational exposure (at the operational level, exposure is the only relevant context). Against this backdrop we conduct a risk assessment. Issues that could affect us in the immediate or near future shape our selection of options for near-term risk mitigation. Probable negative shifts in the operating environment shape our contingency plans for long-term adaptation to the risk environment. We then define initiatives, that is, integrated programmes with specific objectives, to put our plans into action.

NEAR-TERM VERSUS CONTINGENCY PLANS

Note the distinction between near-term risk management plans and long-term contingency plans, which both emerge from the intelligence to action process. For risks that already exist in the operating environment or which we would incur by entering a specific location, we need to be prepared now or very soon. Near-term risk management plans generally focus on avoidance, prevention, and damage limitation through preparation for effective responses to a manifested risk. Such plans are implemented through on-going programmes designed to maintain an appropriate level of preparedness at all times, with our level of preparedness defined by the severity of a risk.

A contingency plan on the other hand, is so called because its implementation is contingent on something happening in the future. In our context, a contingency plan aligns our posture with the emergence of a given scenario. For example, at the project level, a plausible negative three- to five-year scenario might be a 'melt down' of the operating environment: an intermittent civil conflict might blow up or spread to other sub-regions; there might be a dramatic increase in terrorism; and so on. One contingency plan to address this might be exit from the country. Just because we *might* have to exit, it does not mean that we start doing so now. But we can increase our preparation for exit in line with the emergence of the 'melt down' scenario, as identified by monitoring our warnings and indicators.

The ideal contingency plan would enable us to invest just enough in terms of preparation to stay ahead of events without wasting resources in over-preparation, and would have 'back down' points built into it so that a return to normal operations remains an option for as long as possible. In the exit strategy example, if the 'melt down' scenario became active, we might evacuate non-essential staff and equipment, and limit the movement of personnel still on the ground. We might test our emergency evacuation plans to ensure that we are really ready for the emergent stage if it comes. But we do not over-commit by closing down our operation and leaving, and we can easily restore full operations if the situation improves.

Both near-term and contingency plans result in specific implementation initiatives. With near-term risk management, these are on-going programmes which are built into day-to-day operations, while with contingency plans they are more likely to be intermittent reviews followed by discrete projects aimed at adjusting our preparation for a negative future.

RISK INTELLIGENCE: ASSESSMENT VERSUS MONITORING

Risk assessment can be regarded as a rigorous review conducted from a blank slate. It might build on prior knowledge, but if it is not conducted as a fresh exercise, then we risk falling into the trap of expecting more of the same, and potentially missing new and important changes in our operating environment. At the corporate level, a global assessment would reasonably be conducted in alignment with the corporate strategic planning cycle. At the operational level, a top-level assessment would be required in the bid or opportunity assessment phase, then once we commit to an operation and have more information about where and how it will happen, we can expand on the initial assessment with more detailed research. Future assessments would then align with significant phases in the project. When the project profile, and therefore our exposure, changes, we need to conduct a new review taking this into account. Operational level assessments can also be triggered by major changes in the operating environment which alter the risk landscape, rather than our exposure.

Assessments, however, are not the only times when we seek risk intelligence. We need to regularly monitor the risks that we identified in the assessment to ensure that our estimation of their severity remains accurate and up to date, and therefore that our risk management planning is current. In the case of scenarios, we need to keep an eye on our defined warnings and indicators to remain aware of the level of emergence of a scenario, and adjust our contingency plans and preparedness accordingly. The intensity or frequency of monitoring is defined by the severity of a risk, or the plausibility of a negative scenario. The more serious or likely a risk or future state, the more we need to pay attention to it.

While an assessment might result in a weighty report, the outputs of risk monitoring are usually periodic, concise intelligence briefs, and briefings, notifying managers of recent changes in the risk landscape. Monitoring might not lead to new risk management initiatives, but it will lead to useful adjustments which maintain alignment between risk management capability and the evolving political landscape.

POLITICAL RISK MANAGEMENT MEASURES

We can define four broad categories of political risk management measures: portfolio management; security; relationship-building; and risk transfer. We will address each of these in turn, looking in detail at some of the specific measures in each category.

Note that not all of these are relevant to a given company or operation. In practice, risk assessment indicates the specific measures that we need to include as part of our risk management strategy. For an identified risk, we would examine our options for dealing with it, and select those which are most cost effective, not just in terms of addressing that particular risk, but also in terms of potential applicability to other risks. What follows can be regarded as a sample menu.

PORTFOLIO MANAGEMENT

Through an assessment of our global portfolio of operations and investments we arrive at an indication of our global exposure to political risk, and this enables us to adjust the portfolio to achieve our desired overall level of risk. Imagine that our strategy includes a strong element of risk-taking, both to gain the rewards associated with risk, and to stay ahead of our more conservative competitors. However, our political risk portfolio assessment indicates that in fact we have tended to limit most of our operations to low-risk environments, which tend to be highly competitive simply because they are more accessible. We can revise our investment acceptance criteria to favour higher risk environments, and over time our portfolio will shift as old projects in low-risk areas are completed and new operations in higher-risk areas are undertaken.

Similarly, we might find that we are dangerously over-exposed to volatile emerging markets, and given a few major crises we could even face strategic disruption. Again, we can revise our investment criteria to favour less risky environments, and over time the portfolio will become more balanced.

The political risk portfolio assessment, in conjunction with our risk tolerance, effectively informs the 'go/no-go' decision about specific opportunities that we could take on. Every new operation will adjust the portfolio, and if we control which ones we take on, we can tailor our overall level of global risk, and avoid major overexposure.

SECURITY

Security is a broad term for the measures we take to protect ourselves against threats, that is, actors with a specific intention to harm us, and against dangers that exist in the operating environment. We will deal with three specific measures here.

Due diligence investigations   One security sub-measure is due diligence investigations. Due diligence often refers to a detailed assessment of an investment opportunity, but in this context it means discerning vested interests among organisations and people with whom we associate. If risk assessment indicates, for example, a high level of corruption or politically-connected crime in an environment, then we know that we need to be very careful about the relationships we enter into, and due diligence is regularly conducted on prospective relations prior to any commitment. If an investigation indicates that the prospective relation has interests antithetical to our own, or has a reputation that could lead to embarrassment for our own company, then we can either avoid the relationship or tailor it to minimise our exposure.

Due diligence can be necessary at any level, from the strategic to the mundane. A state customer, for example, might be seeking our engagement mainly to gain access to our intellectual property in order to boost national industry without investing heavily in R&D. Or a state enterprise customer might in fact be controlled by regime figures with a track record for criminality or human rights abuses. An investigation could uncover such motives or characteristics and save us potential loss or reputational damage. As another example, a prospective supplier might rely heavily on illegal child labour. If we made a deal with them, then our own supply chain, and therefore the firm generally, would be tainted and

124

subject to ethical recriminations and potentially legal liability. Again an investigation could uncover such risks.

At the mundane level we need to be aware of the real intentions and background of any individual who might gain access to our assets or knowledge of our risk management capabilities. For example, domestic staff in developing countries often come under pressure to provide information about an expatriate's security arrangements to facilitate crime or kidnapping – they might not seem to be in a position to harm us, but unless we know their affiliations they could cause considerable damage. The same can be said of employees whose positions would give them information that could be used to harm us, or access to sensitive intellectual property.

We need not be suspicious as a matter of routine, but when risk assessment indicates that we could be the target of nefarious intentions in a given environment, then due diligence should become a regular part of the process of deciding which relationships we take on, and how to structure them to protect our own interests.

Physical security Physical security seeks the preservation of people and fixed assets, and minimisation of loss, not just in financial terms but also in terms of intellectual property. It can involve, for example: perimeter security and access control to protect installations, homes and offices; IT security; protection of people and assets outside of fixed installations, for example, of travelling expatriates, transport convoys or off-site work crews; and crisis response in the event that harm is incurred, for example, someone is hurt or kidnapped or a natural disaster strikes and causes destruction or injury.

Every firm requires a basic level of security across the board globally, since crime, natural disasters and international terrorism can occur anywhere. Every company also needs to be aware of where its people are when they travel abroad and be capable of supporting them if they encounter hazards. At the operational level, however, security should be tailored for the specific local risk environment, and in unstable areas will likely be much more intense. It is not uncommon for security to pervade all aspects of an operation: expat personnel could routinely be met at the airport by secure escorts and accompanied when moving; there could be an armed guard presence to deter attacks on company assets; a quick reaction force or crisis management capacity might be on call to respond to immediate threats; personnel will have a detailed list of 'dos and don'ts' in terms of keeping themselves safe, including a regularly updated list of 'no-go' areas; and of course evacuation plans and logistics will be designed and tested. It is not uncommon for operations in conflict-prone areas, or areas with a high incidence of terrorism, to allocate as much as 20 per cent of their operating budget to physical security.

Not every foreign operator will be comfortable with the inclusion of military-style measures in their business operations. Some firms balk at the reputational implications of affiliation with armed force and counter-terrorism skills. In some industries and for some corporate cultures, if risk assessment indicates that such measures would be required, then it might be a good indication that risk tolerance has been exceeded and the project should not be pursued in the first place.

For others, however, intensive security is a necessary cost of doing business. This is especially so for the extractive industries and infrastructure constructors, for whom some of the best opportunities lie in volatile environments, and who can only fulfil their projects through the implantation of significant numbers of personnel and heavy equipment over a period of years. It is also increasingly true for logistics firms who often rely on routes which are routinely exposed to armed piracy. Such firms would almost inevitably face a much greater incidence of harm if security was less intense.

In either case, risk assessment will provide advanced notice of the level of security that would be required, and enable a firm to make an informed decision about whether or not it should proceed given that requirement. If a company gets onto the ground without knowing the risks, then security can either be too lax, or else, when managers really sense the risks firsthand, it can be applied as a panic reaction and could well become excessively burdensome and obtrusive in relation to the real level of risk.

Some caveats about physical security are worth noting. For many business managers, physical security seems like a straightforward solution to risk. It is something we can put a price tag on, and it is often governed by commercial contracts with specialist providers who speak the same language of business. However, over-reliance on security for risk management can lead to a company incurring local animousity: 'These people think they need to hide behind their fences, and intimidate us with armed thugs ...'. It can also incur an international reputation for lack of willingness to engage with host communities and interest only in a 'fast buck'. Local animousity towards heavy-handed security in particular can actually increase risk, since it decreases a host community's acceptance of the company, and this can play into the hands of extremist or criminal groups who see the foreign firm as a prospective target. Risk management strategy needs to ensure a careful balance between security and relationship-building to avoid reputational damage and the exacerbation of risk on the ground.

Another necessary balancing act is the one between physical security of the firm, and security of people in the host community. Heavy-handed security can lead to human rights abuses. In some cases a government contract or foreign investment regulations will stipulate that a firm must rely on government forces for security provision, yet in many developing countries such forces have notorious human rights records, and their use in company security can effectively amount to subsidising an abusive state apparatus. Even when international private security firms are used, the risk of collusion in human rights abuses can be significant. One need look no further than the recent Blackwater debacle in Iraq to see how private security can get out of hand, to the detriment of the host community (the facts of the Blackwater case remain open to debate regardless of recent legal rulings, but that the situation arose at all illustrates the risk of obtrusive or heavy-handed security).

An important set of guidelines on how to prevent collusion with abuses is the Voluntary Principles on Security and Human Rights. The Principles were created through a collaborative effort by governments, NGOs and primarily extractive industry firms in 2000, with an eye towards establishing best practice standards in the prevention of abuses by security forces protecting foreign operations. The Principles are best applied through rigorous training of security providers and corporate security managers in what these standards mean and how to comply with them, and routine monitoring of compliance. It is increasingly routine for foreign operators to openly state their compliance with the Principles, allow external auditing and reporting, and in cases where a government insists on providing security, to ensure that contracts stipulate a requirement for security force training and compliance. Abiding by the Principles, or at least the spirit of them, goes a long way towards averting reputational issues associated with security, and can actually make security more effective by adding an important layer of oversight and discipline.

Expatriate security training   The final security sub-measure that we will discuss here is security training for expatriate personnel. The typical Western business manager will have spent most of their life in a familiar setting, at least in cultural and political terms. In developed countries, they will have an embedded understanding of the rules of the game in terms of personal security: what an unsafe neighbourhood looks and feels like; the kinds of areas to avoid; the kinds of personal risks they might face, usually in terms of crime; and what they can expect from the police. They will see elected governments come and go with little impact in terms of the situation 'on the street'. In terms of the workplace and business, the main risks that they will be aware of are white collar crime and issues around discrimination and harassment.

A developing country experiencing a degree of political unrest will be very new terrain. The significance of tradition and custom in personal and business relationships will likely come as a surprise, as well as the higher level of cultural sensitivity. The expat will be unaccustomed to the more intense effect of politics on everyday life, especially in terms of a regime's hostility towards dissent and the fear which that can instil in ordinary people. Politics actually having a violent edge to it, in terms of both regime paranoia and the zero-sum attitude of its opponents, will be new and disquieting.

In addition, the average foreigner from a wealthy country, especially a Western country, will represent an easy target for criminals and scammers confident in the foreigner's ignorance of the local terrain, and a prospective target for extremist groups who regard the foreigner's Western ideological affiliation with hostility. In some cases, even the police might regard the expat as unworthy of their professional support, or opportunistically as a target to be exploited for their own gain.

Security professionals might be on hand, but given the expatriate's inexperience with the new and more risky environment, reliance on external security provision alone is insufficient to keep people safe. They need to make fundamental adjustments to how they see themselves in relation to their environment, and make security an explicit and conscious aspect of their everyday comportment. This calls for new skills and awareness in personal security management.

There are generally three types of personal security training. One is travel security awareness, and is aimed at corporate travellers who routinely travel or work in a range of developing countries. The objective of such training is to provide the traveller or expat worker with a general awareness of the personal risks they face in such environments, and a check-list for their own comportment to ensure their well-being. Such training can be valuable for any traveller who frequents developing regions or anywhere where political unrest is not uncommon.

For long-term assignments in a specific country, country briefings for expat personnel are an added layer of nuance.

Such briefings will build on general travel security awareness by contextualising it for a specific environment in terms of culture, politics, crime, and so on. This will include learning about the security protocols, security management structure, and rules of engagement which the country office has developed for that specific environment. As well, training for long-term assignments includes a higher dose of psychological preparation for culture shock.

The third kind of personal security training is one which is more common among NGOs, journalists and donor development agencies, but which can also be useful to companies operating in particularly conflict-prone settings. This is commonly known as Hazardous Environment Awareness Training (HEAT). Its aim is to prepare people to avoid risk, but also to maximise their chances of coming through even hair-raising situations that could occur on the ground. Training covers areas such as dealing with armed road blocks, dealing with detention or kidnapping, how to take cover and get away from open armed battle, riots or terrorist bombings, and so on. Expats undertaking such training will typically already have some familiarity with unstable environments, and HEAT is used to prepare experienced staff for even less savoury postings. Indeed it should probably only be used for relatively experienced staff. Logically they are the best equipped to send to high-risk environments anyway, and if HEAT training was given to a relative newcomer to international work, there is a risk that the recipient could be traumatised by early exposure to the 'gory details' of operating in the worst kinds of places.

RELATIONSHIP-BUILDING

Relationship-building is a critical and often overlooked political risk management measure. There are two principal aims: gain support in managing political risk; and increased acceptance within host communities.

Gaining politically influential supporters In the first vein, we can use our earlier stakeholder assessment to identify potential politically-influential supporters. These might include particular governments, state agencies, transnational organisations or NGOs who regard our success as compatible with their interests. It could even include, at the operational level, specific individuals within the host government, for example, those who regard our investment as important to long-term economic development, and who see foreign investors generally as valuable development partners.

Friendly stakeholders can help us in a variety of ways. One of these is information. Relationships with political actors can give us first-hand insights into the political environment, and provide an early warning of shifts in policy or government attitude which could affect us. They can also warn us of intensifying conflict or unrest, usually on the basis of direct access to classified national intelligence.

Friendly stakeholders can also provide counterweights to potentially hostile influences. In the example of a construction project aimed at a new airport terminal in a North African capital, the Ministry of Transport might regard our operation favourably because of the unique skills that we will transfer in the course of the operation, but the Ministry of Trade might have been cultivating investment ties with China and resent our having won the contract instead of a Chinese bidder.

Left to its own devices, and in the context of weak governance, the Trade Ministry would take every opportunity to set up bureaucratic and regulatory obstacles to our success, in order to validate their initial choice of a Chinese supplier. But given the Transport Ministry's influence within the central government, it can easily counter such obstacles and help pave the way for a smooth operation.

Another form of support is liaison. A friendly political stakeholder can act as a bridge or communications channel between the company and other important but unapproachable stakeholders. For example, the Transport Ministry above could be a useful conduit between our firm and the executive level of the regime. The regime might initially regard us with suspicion and might be supportive of the stance of the Trade Ministry, but if the Transport Minister is pleased with our work, he can convey good reports to the regime and thereby increase its support for our operation. Another example particularly pertinent to extractive firms operating in conflict-prone settings is using friendly NGOs or local officials for liaison with insurgent groups. For example, a local insurgent group might initially be hostile to our presence, and this could lead to attacks. But if a stakeholder who understands our operations well explains to the group that our presence is likely to benefit the local community, then this hostility can be mitigated.

Relationships with political actors always need to be handled with care. If a company is perceived as a political actor itself, it will be treated as such, and this far exceeds most firms' comfort zones and competencies. We also need to stringently avoid a reputation for being manipulative or conniving, and avoid any association with corruption in the course of developing relationships.

Acceptance Gaining acceptance is the other objective of relationship-building. The aim is to reduce risk by increasing the acceptance of the firm as a responsible and valuable player in the international arena and in specific operating environments. Acceptance minimises potential friction and maximises the chances of cooperation between the firm and its political stakeholders. This is a broad domain, but we can capture the concept through reference to a few principal sub-measures.

One is compliance with regulatory and ethical standards relevant to the firm's business and operating environments. Regulatory compliance ensures that the firm does not incur friction with relevant governments and transnational political organisations. All international companies will need to consider home and host country regulations relevant to their business. But they also need to be aware of specific national and international regulations which, although enforceable within a specific jurisdiction, have evolved into global standards. Most global standards govern transparency and accountability in accounting practices and financial risk management (for example, The US Generally Accepted Accounting Priciples [GAAP], Basel II, Sarbanes Oxley, and so on), or corruption (for example, the US Foreign Corrupt Practices Act), but there are other areas relevant to specific sectors.

Ethical, as opposed to regulatory, standards might not be enforceable by law, but several such standards are becoming benchmarks by which global corporate citizenship is gauged. These include, for example, the UN Global Compact, the OECD Convention on Anti-Bribery, the Equator Principles (concerning the social and environmental implications of project financing), and the Extractive Industries Transparency Initiative (concerning transparency in the expenditure of national revenues derived from oil and mineral extraction). A company will often have the choice of either becoming a signatory to such standards, in which case they will be expected to demonstrate compliance, or interpreting the spirit of such standards and integrating them into wider corporate governance. In either case, adherence to at least the spirit of global ethical standards enhances one's position as a globally responsible business.

A more proactive acceptance measure can be summarised as communication and consultation. At the global level this means maintaining an open dialogue with civil society to understand their expectations and interests in terms of the firm's strategy and behaviour, and to ensure that civil society representatives understand the business imperatives of the firm. Strategy and operational comportment can then be tailored to obtain a reasonable degree of alignment between global social needs and business imperatives.

In terms of specific actors to be consulted, on the government side these would include donor agencies of national governments heavily involved in international development, transnational organisations which represent the interests of specific regions or tiers of developing countries (for example, the Organisation for African Unity [OAU]), and international NGOs with a well established reputation for setting ethical standards in their domain of concern, for example, human rights, development, or environmental protection. At the operational level host government agencies relevant to the operation, mainstream local NGOs and local representatives of international development agencies and global NGOs would be the focus of communication.

One caveat in communication and consultation is that unless a company periodically acts on the insights obtained through such interaction, it can appear to be a cynical publicity exercise. A corollary of this, of course, is that companies should manage expectations carefully – in the end a company is a profit-seeking entity with necessary growth imperatives, and its very existence as a viable economic actor is itself a value to society. Consultation and communications are a necessary means of ensuring reasonable alignment with civil society perspectives, but a company needs to be careful not to imply that the communications process will in fact define its strategy, or it will be setting itself up for failure in the eyes of civil society observers.

The term 'Corporate Social Responsibility' (CSR) is often applied to acceptance more broadly, or at least those elements of it which pertain to relationships with civil society. We will apply a more narrow definition for our purposes: CSR is the firm's way of off-setting hardship caused by its business by tailoring operations for minimal negative impact on host communities, and by directly contributing to the long-term well-being of communities in its operating environments. At the global level, CSR can take the form of active participation in and financial contribution to international initiatives aimed at sustainable development, for example, disease-reduction campaigns, 'green' energy initiatives and initiatives to align sustainable development imperatives and global investment patterns. Such participation ensures that the firm has a voice in initiatives which could affect it, and contributes to the firm's reputation as a globally responsible entity with an interest in its effect on society.

At the operational level CSR can mean a similar form of participation in regional or country-specific initiatives, but it also means social investment in communities directly affected by company operations. Such initiatives usually follow from a social–environmental impact assessment which feeds not only into the technical design of the project to ensure minimal environmental impact, but also informs the firm of its probable impact on the socio-economic structure of the host community. Operational CSR initiatives include, for example, support for micro-finance schemes, renewable food sources, local education/job training, sanitation, and, in less stable environments, for inter-community peace-building. The net effect of operational CSR is that communities affected by business operations are better off through their exposure to the firm.

A significant caveat in operational CSR is that a company's direct interaction with the affected community can incur problems. A foreign firm will probably lack a sufficient understanding of the cultural nuances and local rivalries that exist on the ground. If it directly engages with host communities, it risks cultural rejection of its initiatives and the exacerbation of local rivalries if some groups are perceived to benefit more than others. The solution is to develop partnerships with reputable local NGOs and experienced international development agencies which have an intrinsic understanding of local society, and to let them lead as the principal liaison with the host community. The company can work with these intermediaries to ensure that CSR initiatives achieve the desired effect, without directly exposing the firm to sensitivities which it could not reasonably anticipate.

Somewhere between host country regulatory compliance and CSR at the operational level is adherence with local content imperatives. Many host governments will have regulations in place which require that foreign operators rely whenever possible on local labour and suppliers, in order to ensure economic benefits for the host society, and to accelerate development through building job skills and technology transfer. Compliance with regulations is a minimum target for the foreign operator, but on the CSR side, local content initiatives can be enhanced to help ensure that the benefits of the firm's presence have sustainable effects into the future. For example, local content activities can be designed in synchronisation with support for micro-finance and educational development within the wider community.

Local content regulations have presented headaches. An international firm might already know where it would source skilled workers and dependable suppliers on the global or regional market, and having to source these again at the local level can represent delays. Quality of local skills and products in developing countries can also be far below what a firm is accustomed to. Local content should be carefully taken into account in the original design of a contract to allow for possible additional costs and delays, and when local content is insufficient for certain operational requirements, then the firm needs to negotiate alternatives in those areas.

In the end though, a foreign business needs to recognise that one main reason for local content in the first place is the skills and quality gap between developed and developing countries. Local content regulations are indeed one way to address this gap, and for the host country it has the advantage of being applied in a real commercial context, not as an abstract development initiative led by foreign donors.

The last acceptance sub-measure which we will discuss here is conflict sensitivity. This means taking socio-political conflict into account in the design of business investments and operations so that the company does not inadvertently exacerbate conflict. At the global level this can mean factoring in international rivalries when deciding on new geographic growth targets. When operations in one country would likely contribute to suspicion and a sense of vulnerability in another, the firm's decisions could be a factor in increasing international tensions. For example, recently a European firm pulled out of key projects in Iran because of Israeli and Arab Gulf concerns that they would have significantly enhanced Iran's capacity to extend its military reach in the region. Defence firms need to take special care in this respect, but any company involved in infrastructure, communications or energy development can also inadvertently augment a country's strategic reach at the expense of rival nations.

Conflict sensitivity at the operational level needs to consider the foreign business impact on government human rights abuses, civil conflict and community tensions. First, government revenues derived from foreign participation in state contracts can increase funds available for arms or for buying off political rivals. This can reduce a government's willingness to seek negotiated solutions to civil conflict, and increase its abusive capacity vis-à-vis civil society. A recent example of this is foreign investment in Chad's oil production. It appears that rather than contributing to national development, the revenues accruing from increased oil output have made an already unsavoury regime even less tractable (note that the Extractive Industries Transparency Initiative was created to address this kind of situation).

Second, investments which contribute to the well-being of one group or region in a country, especially at the expense of others, can exacerbate civil conflict. This has been especially problematic in Nigeria. Oil investment in the Delta region has caused considerable hardship for Delta communities in terms of environmental decay, yet other provinces in the country tend to benefit more from the Delta's oil revenues which are controlled and redistributed by the central government. The result has been a long-standing insurgency in the Delta, with oil firms as regular targets.

Finally, even within specific national sub-regions or communities, a perception that a foreign firm's presence is unfairly augmenting the well-being of some groups and ignoring others can inflame local tensions and stir up low-level conflict.

At the operational level a company needs to ensure that it knows the conflict environment on the ground, in terms of axes of friction and divergent stakeholders, and tailors its operation for minimal conflict exacerbation. In the contract design phase, this could mean ensuring host country government guarantees in terms of the equitable use of project revenues: this is best done with the support of influential multi-lateral or donor government lenders. It can also mean ensuring that benefits from employment and CSR initiatives are spread equally between affected sub-communities and that the company clearly communicates its policy of focusing mainly on communities which endure the most hardship as a result of the project, so that other groups understand why they might not be benefiting to the same degree. The company's own comportment with respect to cultural sensitivity and unobtrusive security are also relevant factors under the firm's control. Finally, as part of CSR, the firm can actively support peace-building initiatives.

Conflict sensitivity really has two benefits. One is in terms of acceptance. A firm that does not exacerbate tensions, thereby decreasing human security in its operating environments, is clearly a more responsible and socially conscious player. Second, by avoiding making conflict worse and by actively supporting peace-building, a company is actually reducing risks to its personnel and performance by contributing to a more stable environment in which the firm itself is less likely to become a victim of violence.

RISK TRANSFER

This is the final main political risk management measure, and is aimed at reducing the firm's risk by sharing it with other stakeholders.

One transfer mechanism is project finance structures which give a major donor country or transnational lending organisation (for example, the World Bank) a stake in a project. In some cases the lender will have already identified the requirement for the project, perhaps at the behest of a recipient government, and the funding will be available to the firm who meets the tender requirements. In other cases, the company might identify the opportunity and seek lenders to back the host government customer.

In either case the company has the opportunity to ensure that the lender takes on some of the hazards associated with political risk, most directly in terms of government behaviour with respect to contract fulfilment, payment and failure to complete the project because of an untenable political environment.

Another measure is of course insurance, whereby the firm purchases a package of policies designed to protect the firm from losses associated with political risk. Assets covered tend to be related to people and business performance, the latter mainly with respect to government behaviour in contract fulfilment and payment, expropriation, terrorism and war.

It is important to note that most political insurance covers the more tangible business assets and the more observable, measureable risks. There is a lot of grey space which even the best political risk insurance package will leave without cover, and some assets, such as reputation or morale, are simply not quantifiable. Furthermore, insurance might cover against tangible loss, but having insurance is no guarantee of success: it does not cover failure to achieve strategic ambition. Insurance is therefore best seen as a way to hedge against loss where it is possible to do so cost-effectively, and as a partial enabler of risk-taking, not as a means of succeeding in risky global initiatives.

It is worth noting that in both project financing and insurance, there are non-transfer benefits to using government and transnational-backed lenders and guarantors. Major donors and their respective lending and guarantee agencies carry considerable weight with developing country governments, who often rely on the same donors for long-term loans and development assistance. If the donor might be harmed through host government action, it can therefore bring much more bargaining power to bear than the average corporation, and host governments are far more wary of not living up to their obligations when donors have a stake. Private insurers tend to be more flexible and cover a wider array of risks, but this needs to be balanced by the strategic advantages of donor backing.

Another transfer mechanism is partnerships with other firms who will bear the risk for certain phases or elements of a project. If, for example, a European constructor won a contract to build a new terminal at a North African airport, the constructor could subcontract certain sites, services or installations (for example, electrical equipment) to other firms who would bear the risk for their own sub-projects. Partnerships can be beneficial in other ways too. A partner might have much more experience in the given region and better relationships, or their brand and national background might be more respected. This contributes to acceptance. They might also already have well-adapted security approaches to risk in unstable areas, and the principal firm could apply these to its own assets, or at least learn better approaches from the sub-contractor.

Finally, it is possible to design contracts with host governments and state enterprises to transfer part of the risk back onto them. When risk assessment indicates a risk of expropriation or pressure on foreign control generally, a contract, and indeed the entire project, should be designed to hold back or limit state customer access to key intellectual property or technologies, with transfer of anything critical to project completion happening as late as possible in the project cycle, and payment staged with project phases. The state will therefore have little incentive to expropriate the project. It will gain little and save little through expropriation, and will face the implications of an uncompleted project. The company can thereby maintain some control over the bargain for the duration or large part of the project.

ORGANISATIONAL STRUCTURES

This section examines the structures that a company can build to guide and implement political risk management at the global and operational levels. We begin with a consideration of the leadership function, then examine how political risk management initiatives can be structured, and finally consider the relevance of traditional management functions to political risk management, and therefore their availability as political risk management resources.

LEADERSHIP AND GUIDANCE

Corporate It is probably clear from the above explanation of the measures of political risk management that there is unlikely to be a single management function or department which covers all relevant skills. Indeed, posing the question, 'Who handles political risk in your company?' often yields blank stares. This easily leads to a situation in which people across an organisation are dealing with political risk in their own niche terms, often at cross-purposes with other departments or functions. With the stakes involved, this is far from optimal.

Given that the skills necessary to deal with political risk usually are embodied in existing management functions, adding yet another layer of management in the form of a hefty political risk department seems redundant. However, there is a clear need for leadership on this unique and cross-functional challenge to ensure a coherent organisational response. To this end, we suggest the creation of a small but authoritative leadership team, acting as the hub of expertise on political risk, and leading in the development of risk management approaches and assessments.

The political risk leadership team would ideally consist of representatives of the Board, a senior executive with direct oversight of the function, and a small, permanent, team of analysts and planners. Board representation is necessary not only for visibility, but because in the end political risk management is a governance function. It represents potentially significant value depletion and therefore failure to meet obligations to shareholders and social stakeholders. A senior executive, on the other hand, understands day-to-day operations from a strategic perspective and can ensure that political risk management is integrated into enterprise risk management processes, strategic planning and business execution. A small but permanent analytical team is required in order to provide the intellectual and research capacity that underlies the development of best practice and political risk assessments, and to act as internal consultants on political risk for operational managers.

Board representation should include directors with both considerable experience in international business, and a strong interest in the issue. Their role would be to provide guidance and oversight, and to ensure that political risk has visibility at the Board level.

A natural choice for the executive head of the team might seem to be the Chief Risk Officer (CRO), but in many cases CROs have more experience in insurance, risk finance and enterprise risk management than in high-risk international operations. The Chief Operating Officer (COO) could be better positioned, since they would have a broader perspective on day-to-day operations and ultimate oversight of international growth initiatives. The Vice-President of International Operations, if there is one, might be ideal. The role of the team leader would be to steer relevant policy development, oversee the political risk management planning process, and oversee evaluations of political risk management performance and improvement initiatives. They would also work to ensure that political risk had visibility among the executive leadership and operating departments.

The permanent analytical support team would ideally consist of a mixture of backgrounds reflecting different perspectives on political risk, for example, strategy, risk management, international affairs, and international operations. This team would directly undertake or source political risk assessments and monitoring intelligence, develop internal political risk management practices and policy, lead on political risk management performance evaluations (with the team leader's oversight), and act in an internal liaison and consulting capacity to ensure consistency in political risk management across the firm.

Another important element of establishing political risk in the corporate mind-set would be the structured participation of other management functions in initiatives aimed at developing and improving political risk management practices. In many corporations, managers and personnel have their regular line jobs, but also participate in cross-departmental initiatives, such as new venture development or process optimisation. Political risk management can easily become another such axis of collaboration. Under the guidance of the leadership team, members of this cross-functional 'task force' would help to improve the understanding of political risk in their own departments, and to ensure alignment with emerging best practice. Their participation would also send a strong signal that this is not an arcane specialist field, but something of relevance to all participants in international operations.

One of the key responsibilities of the leadership team would be to develop an appropriate political risk management policy. Once 'live', this document would form tangible reference points for consistency in political risk management across the firm, and would serve as a useful educative tool. A policy document would include, for example:

- The concept of political risk and the objectives of political risk management.

- The firm's own philosophy on political risk, as defined by corporate strategy, culture, and risk tolerance.

- A synopsis of the key risks that the firm faces at the global level, and a snapshot of the kinds of issues facing overseas operations.

- The political risk management process and key risk management measures.

- The roles that executives and operating departments can play in addressing political risk.

- How and when to collaborate on political risk management in terms of joint initiatives at the corporate and operational levels, and information-sharing.

- Guidelines for the creation of political risk management initiatives at the operational and country levels.

- How to participate in the wider corporate political management endeavour (definition of practices and processes).

- An appendix with additional resources, such as key assessment tools, risk intelligence sources, and so on.

This document should be freely available within the firm, and could also be used to guide partners and other collaborators in how to align their own political risk management practices with that of the company. Together, a permanent leadership team, structured inter-departmental collaboration, and a widely disseminated policy put political risk management on the corporate map as a tangible and valuable function.

Operational Political risk management at the country or operational level would have its own presence, and for the same reasons that apply at the corporate level it would need to be just as explicit.

A key difference at the operational level is that the operating unit is smaller, more integrated, its members in closer physical proximity to each other, and everyone is reasonably familiar with the same discrete operating environment. Alignment and collaboration around political risk is therefore much easier, and risk management can be built into the operation as a tacit element of every relevant management function.

The country or project manager would take the lead. Based on prior operational risk assessment and with the support of the corporate political risk team, they would develop an appropriate political risk management strategy for their specific project or country operation. This would be divided into discrete initiatives which could then be assigned to the relevant functions on the ground. The heads of these initiatives and the country/project manager would form the political risk management team for the project, although the corporate team would retain an advisory role and participate in initiatives requiring dedicated political risk expertise.

The crucial point in establishing political risk management at the operational level is that it is explicitly recognised as a necessary management function. This can be a challenge. First, there would not be an independent entity on the ground called the 'political risk team' to ensure that the issue remains top of mind. Second, country and project teams are often under intense pressure to deliver on time and on budget, and tend to minimise attention to anything but immediate project objectives. This is fine as long as nothing goes wrong, but in an environment rife with the potential for complications, it is inviting problems. It would be part of the corporate team's function to ensure that managers of international operations understand the criticality of political risk management, and explicitly factor it into their planning and day-to-day work.

STRUCTURING POLITICAL RISK MANAGEMENT INITIATIVES

The tangible approach to political risk at the global or operational level will be an integrated set of initiatives, or programmes, designed to address priority risks and to prepare for future contingencies.

The first step in developing relevant initiatives is to group risks into manageable sets according to common issues they pose. Developing a different approach to each separate risk can lead to unworkable complexity and redundancy, and it is likely that several risks can be managed by a single integrated approach, thereby making the most of available resources. For example, a risk assessment might indicate terrorism, violent crime and violent civil unrest as priority risks. Rather than dealing with each one separately, we can deal with the common challenge which they present: threat to personnel. In so doing, we address the wider challenge and ensure maximum synergy between specific risk management activities, that is, anything we do to mitigate the risk of violent crime, for example, can be designed to have a mitigating effect on the risks of unrest and terrorism, and vice versa.

Next we assign a lead function to handle each set of risks. The lead function is selected on the basis of the relevance of its expertise to the given set of risks. For threat to personnel, the logical choice, for example, would be the security function. The security manager will be responsible for designing and managing an appropriate programme to address this issue. The logic of initiative definition is captured in Figure 5.2.

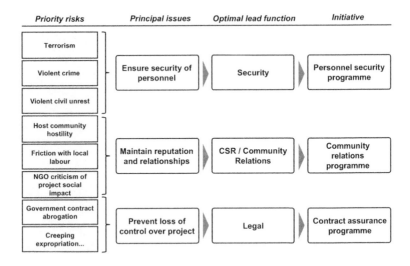

Priority risks	Principal issues	Optimal lead function	Initiative
Terrorism / Violent crime / Violent civil unrest	Ensure security of personnel	Security	Personnel security programme
Host community hostility / Friction with local labour / NGO criticism of project social impact	Maintain reputation and relationships	CSR / Community Relations	Community relations programme
Government contract abrogation / Creeping expropriation...	Prevent loss of control over project	Legal	Contract assurance programme

Figure 5.2   Defining political risk management initiatives

After defining a programme, the lead function will know what other kinds of expertise are required for effective implementation. The lead function then recruits a programme team on this basis, integrating other relevant functions as required to provide all of the necessary expertise. The input of these subordinate functions will vary between providing ongoing support to acting in an on-call advisory capacity, but all of them will explicitly be members of the programme team.

It is very likely that a lead function on one issue will also be a supporting member in other programme teams. The total approach to political risk management is likely to be linked by cross-membership of different functions in different initiatives. This is not only a natural outcome of the process of defining initiatives, but it ensures that initiatives do not become narrow silos of activity that can end up working at cross purposes, and that all personnel involved have a top-level perspective of the total political risk management approach, and hence the relevance of their own role within it. The concept of cross-membership is illustrated in Figure 5.3. Note that this is drawn from the operational level, and that only a few relevant functions are illustrated.

All initiatives will be overseen by the relevant political risk team (corporate or country), who will ensure coherence and balance, and that there are not any gaps or redundancies in addressing priority risks. The political risk team will also ensure that each initiative has reasonable and verifiable performance goals, and will troubleshoot when these goals are not met.

As this chapter makes clear, political risk management is not a specialist domain, rather a diverse function which cross-cuts traditional management functions and departments. It is useful to depict the role that different traditional functions can play in political risk management, thereby indicating potentially relevant internal resources when it comes to structuring initiatives. These functions include, but are not limited to:

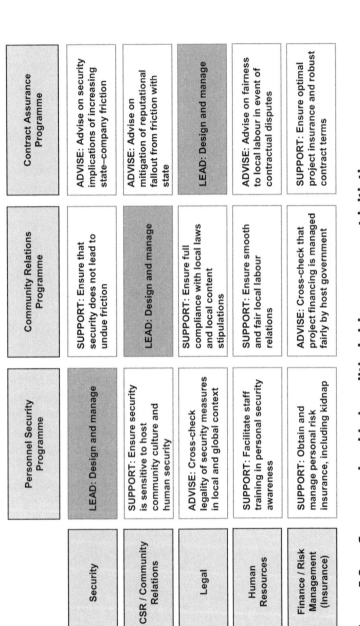

Figure 5.3   Cross-membership in political risk management initiatives

- Security and Health and Safety. Physical protection, safety and loss prevention, and leading in due diligence investigations.

- Risk Management (as traditionally defined in most corporations). Definition of insurance and financial risk management requirements, acquisition of relevant insurance services, and internal audit to ensure corporate integrity and compliance with relevant regulations.

- External Relations. Oversight of the regulatory environment and direct interaction with government and public stakeholders to cultivate on-going relationships, and to ensure open communication about mutual interests and concerns.

- Community Relations/CSR (this function sometimes falls under External Relations but would ideally be separate if a firm regularly works on the ground in sensitive environments). Assessment of the socio-environmental impact of business operations, and definition and oversight of CSR programmes aimed at supporting communities affected by business operations.

- Legal. Oversight of contract design and leading on contractual negotiations to ensure mutual fairness and to take into account risks of default by contracting authorities, as well as assessing the legality of specific risk management measures.

- Human Resources. In conjunction with Security/Health and Safety, preparation of expatriate personnel for overseas assignments; in conjunction with Risk Management, definition of personal insurance requirements for expat personnel; and labour relations in overseas projects.

- International Marketing and Corporate Strategy (as two separate functions working in conjunction). Consideration of risk tolerance and the global political risk portfolio in development of overseas growth plans, and of the risk–reward equation when considering opportunities in potentially unstable areas.

- Logistics. Design and adjustment of supply chains with consideration to political risk in transit areas.

- Corporate Executive Team and the Board. Oversight of compliance with good governance and corporate citizenship, and ensuring that political risk is factored into corporate strategic decisions.

- Operations. Consideration of political risk management requirements and ensuring compliance with relevant policy in day to day operations.

All of these functions, and likely more, would work with and under the guidance of the corporate political risk team or the country/operational risk team when involved in political risk management.

EVALUATING POLITICAL RISK MANAGEMENT PERFORMANCE

Evaluating risk management performance in any domain, whether financial, operational or political risk-related, is inherently tricky. Unlike normal business performance, risk management is not measuring success in making things happen, but the absence or mitigation of negative effects. If nothing bad happens, is this evidence of sound risk management, or just good luck? There are substantive approaches that can be used, however, to give a reasonable indication of how well we are managing political risk.

One which is common to risk management endeavours is attribution of loss analysis. This is usually a financial estimate, which in political risk terms means that the evaluation pertains mainly to the performance asset. In a nutshell, loss across a firm or operation is aggregated and then analysed to discern the causes of loss and to attribute different levels to different causes. In an international firm, inevitably some loss will be attributable to political risk. Political risk management performance, then, can be assessed as a reduction in the amount of loss caused by political risk in relation to past benchmarks.

Political risk management performance can also assessed through an analysis of the company's reputation with key political stakeholders, including governments, transnational organisations, NGOs and civil society groups. One approach is to track mentions of the firm or a specific project in the press, and in reports issued by NGOs and donor governments. Sound political risk management would be indicated by an absence of severely negative ethical or political criticism, and ideally by generally favourable reviews. Media tracking can be augmented with direct interaction with stakeholders through routine consultation and communication.

An indirect approach to assessing political risk management performance is benchmarking against best-practice firms in one's sector or operating environments. When a company performs well it is generally open to sharing information on its practices, and industry forums and reports often attempt to capture what strongly performing firms do. This information can shape benchmarks. Another option is to utilise consultants who work with a variety of firms in one or several sectors. They could apply their aggregate experience with other companies to form appropriate comparative benchmarks for the organisation undertaking the exercise. The firm can then assess itself against best practice, and identify critical gaps which could lead to underperformance.

Another approach, and one that goes hand in hand with the implementation of political risk management, is the analysis of incident reports. As part of general good practice in risk management, when the company or operation encounters manifested risk, that is, a negative event, those who experienced the encounter first-hand log the event and its outcome, with a summary of lessons learned from the experience. Over time a track record of incidents will accumulate and can be analysed to assess the frequency and seriousness of manifested risks, and performance in dealing with them (that is, mitigating their impacts).

A rather tactical but still indispensable evaluation method is risk simulations. These yield insights into the adeptness of a specific team or management structure in dealing with either specific risks that manifest, or the unexpectedly rapid evolution of a given operating environment.

In the early stages, simulations are learning tools which help teams and individuals to identify gaps in their ability to deal with risk, and give live practice to hone risk management skills. After a firm has some track record in exposure to political risk, simulations can take a more evaluative form, and at least some should be conducted with no prior warning (although with notification that it is just a drill, otherwise apathy might set in and damage performance in real crises, that is,

'It's probably just another drill'). An aggregated analysis of several such exercises can contribute to an assessment of the firm's political risk management performance. For example, if most simulations conducted over the course of a year indicate confusion, procrastination, poor communications or a lack of resources to directly mitigate a risk on the ground, then there would clearly be room for overall improvement.

Simulations have been most commonly applied by the security function, focusing on such risks as the onset of rioting or violent unrest, a terrorist bombing in the vicinity of an operation, or a kidnapping. However, they could usefully be applied to less immediate issues, such as organised criminal pressure or pressure for kickbacks, and also to the emergence of negative scenarios.

It is possible to monitor compliance with political risk management policy through the assessment of documentation and logs which should be produced as part of the implementation process. At the individual level, it would be possible to monitor the usage of risk intelligence available to all international personnel, perhaps through activity logs for those portions of the Intranet which house risk intelligence. The same could be done for utilisation of on-line tools to log travel itineraries and personal travel security plans. At the organisational level, the depth and relevance of risk management planning documents would be available for assessment. Finally, structured management and employee surveys could be used to assess overall awareness of political risk and compliance with relevant policy.

There is no one tool, then, for evaluating political risk management performance. Instead, the outputs of each available tool need to be taken into account, and the types of data which they can provide will help to shape observable/ measureable performance indicators. The following is a hypothetical illustration of performance goals and indicators taking the different evaluative tools into account:

- Reduction in loss attributable to political risk/contribution of political risk management to loss prevention: as measured by loss attribution analysis.

- Reduction in reputational decline attributable to political risk/political risk management's contribution to reputation: as measured by stakeholder perceptions of the company's socio-political performance.

- Alignment with best practice in political risk management in our sector and operating regions: as measured by comparative benchmarking exercises.

- A reduction in the frequency of incidents of manifested risk, and performance in risk impact mitigation: as measured by incident reports.

- Continual improvement in performance in risk simulations: as measured through the accumulated track record in simulation exercises.

- Awareness of/compliance with relevant policy: as measured through tracking of usage of on-line risk intelligence and personal travel portals, assessment of risk management planning documentation, and structured employee surveys.

The net evaluation will therefore need to balance different kinds of information, but having different data sources helps to ensure that all relevant levels of political risk management are evaluated, and that evaluation does not rely on just a top-line figure which could skew the nuanced realities that exist at ground level.

POLITICAL RISK MANAGEMENT STRATEGY

A useful conclusion to this chapter is a consideration of the concept of a political risk management strategy. Thus far we have considered specific measures and the structures that can be built to implement them, but we should not fall into the trap of thinking about the issue in terms of a series of reactive stopgaps. Political risk can be dealt with strategically, and every company needs to shape its approach in the context of its business aspirations and unique corporate culture.

A political risk management strategy can be defined as a company's unique long-term approach to dealing with political risk. It provides the parameters that shape our approach to risk in any given context. The strategy consists of the balance between the four main political risk management measures (portfolio management, security, relationship-building and risk transfer), and aligns our approach to risk with our international growth strategy and desired corporate identity.

Take, for example, two international construction companies. One of them aggressively pursues opportunities wherever they arise, and it sees itself as hard-headed, practical and fiercely competitive. The company seeks maximal agility and maintains the lowest possible overheads. Its strategy for political risk reflects its character and ambitions. The firm transfers as much risk as possible to insurers and partners, and outsources all security and risk intelligence to a major international supplier. In operations, it insists that expat personnel remain on secured sites and minimise interaction with the host community to reduce exposure as much as possible. The firm allocates only enough to CSR to directly offset its own negative effects on host communities, and generally handles CSR by providing lump sum donations to local NGOs, rather than taking an active role in CSR planning. The company regards its success as a business to be its principal value to society, and carefully controls expectations of its social performance. This formula has worked, and enables the agility which is core to the company's strategy.

The second company, on the other hand, has a considerable track record in the Middle East and Africa, and feels a deep affinity to these regions. It invests heavily in cultivating regional and local relationships, and listens carefully to political stakeholders. It is proud to be an accepted presence in its operating countries, and actively supports interaction between its expats and host communities. Expatriates are prepared for assignments with considerable cultural training, in addition to security awareness which enables them to interact securely with host communities. The company uses security consultants and advisers, but retains in-house management of the security function to ensure that security is aligned to the firm's carefully cultivated image. The company takes an active role in CSR programmes designed not just to offset its own impact, but to reinforce its status as an active member of the societies in which it operates. The company has thereby made acceptance in its operating regions a key lynchpin of its political risk management strategy.

Both approaches work, but they are by no means interchangeable. If the two firms were to adopt each other's strategies, they would suddenly find political risk management to be a major impediment to their business strategy and desired corporate identity.

Some measures of political risk management will be fundamentally necessary for any firm in a specific operating environment or context, but there is still considerable room to tailor the balance and nuance of risk management. When exploring approaches to political risk, a company should consider not only its risk tolerance but should ask itself 'What are we trying to achieve and how do we want to be perceived? What risk management strategy is the best one in our unique context?' We can draw a useful comparison to corporate or business unit strategy. Any business needs to grow and be profitable, but no two businesses achieve these in the same way. What works for one company might not work for another even in the same sector. And like business strategy, political risk management strategy needs to be regularly reviewed to ensure that it evolves in line with external realities and does not ossify over time.

(6) Food for Thought

OVERVIEW

We began with an introduction of the concept of political risk, and its relevance to international businesses. Next we examined some of the key risks that companies have encountered, and how the political landscape of business is evolving. Chapter 3 broke the concept of political risk into its constituent analytical variables, including sources of risk and the assets which an international player exposes to new political terrain. Next we examined the political risk assessment process, which derives priority issues for risk management. Chapter 5 then considered how political risk management is conducted, including the principal measures we can utilise and the structures that enable consistent implementation. In this chapter we conclude with several less tangible but still critical questions that cross-cut these substantive chapters.

THE RELEVANCE OF POLITICAL RISK

The preceding chapters have, at various points, made the case for the relevance of political risk to international business. This has been in counterpoint to the frequently encountered perception there is a distinct separation between the domains of business and politics. A business exists to generate legitimate profit, while a political entity's raison d'être is the attainment or influence of authority by which to spread or perpetuate a given social vision. In this perspective, politics is just another and very abstract aspect of the greater landscape within which a business operates.

This perspective tends to derive from international businesses' long experience in developed countries with enduring and stable political institutions and strong governance. In such countries, the separation of business and politics appears to be clearly defined. We do not see many businesses actively participating in the creation of law or major debates around social vision, aside from providing their perspectives through structured consultations. Yet even in such societies, business occurs within a framework defined by political actors, and the pursuit of profit as a legitimate goal was at some point recognised and accepted by political actors as contributing to social value. That the framework and general agreement about the social value of business has gone unchanged for centuries in many 'home markets' has led to companies taking the political backdrop of business for granted, and this has resulted in the perception of a separation between the two domains.

Globalisation has driven businesses beyond locations where this separation can be taken for granted. In many emerging markets, there is little distinction between business and politics, and many political actors are also active members of the business community. Political institutions and perspectives are still being shaped, and there is seldom so definite and enduring a political framework for business as in developed countries. Ideological perceptions of the value and sanctity of private business can shift quite easily in these circumstances, with dramatic effects for business legitimacy, and therefore legal protection. On top of this, given the stakes as competing social visions vie to lay the foundations of the social order, politics does not occur just inside political institutions. It often occurs in the street, manifesting as unrest, repression, insurgency and terrorism. It therefore has a direct impact on the environment in which companies operate, often with tangible effects.

Politics is therefore relevant to international business, and it is indeed because of this that we recognise the concept of political risk in the first place. Risk to what? Business. The corollary of this is that political risk management is relevant to international business performance. Given that we can no longer take the political environment for granted, we need to explicitly manage our interaction with it in order to succeed in our search for legitimate profit. Competency in political risk management therefore becomes an enabler of international business. It preserves a company's assets from harm, thereby enabling success in specific operations, and at the global level it allows us to approach new opportunities with the confidence that we will be prepared to foresee and deal with political risk.

Political risk is relevant the more we operate in emerging markets, and can well be regarded as a significant business enabler and axis of competition in this era of accelerating globalisation.

POLITICAL RISK AS A MANAGEABLE VARIABLE

A corollary of the perception that business and politics are distinctly separate domains is that political risk is somewhat like the weather. It is an exogenous variable that lies largely beyond our control, and worrying about it distracts management attention from the core business pursuit of profitable growth. In this perspective, the best and perhaps only way to handle political risk is insurance. We cannot control what happens, but we can cover our losses against bad things happening, just as we would handle the weather or natural disasters. Even if something goes wrong, we will not lose too much and will live to fight another day, and we will not dither around the issue in the meantime.

We have seen in Chapters 4 and 5 that political risk is not unmanageable. First, with intelligence and analysis, it is possible to obtain actionable insight about the political trends and conditions that could have the most effect on our business. Second, there is an extensive range of measures that we can take to manage risk, and we can structure these as appropriate to significantly mitigate the most relevant risks. Finally, as opposed to being a niche and specialist function, political risk management cross-cuts many traditional management functions. We might need to call on dedicated experts now and then, but on the whole we already have the expertise to manage political risk. The issue is indeed manageable. Unlike the weather, political risk is after all ultimately posed by people, and as people we have a clear opportunity to interact with our political environment, to understand others' motives, needs and capabilities, and to tailor our activities to take these into account.

The approach of hedging against loss, then, might be a necessary element of political risk management strategy, but we sell ourselves far short by making it the major one. It might enable us to survive manifested political risk more or less intact, but it does not protect our less tangible but still critical assets from harm, nor does it help us to succeed in specific initiatives. The best insurance policy will not bring back a skilled manager who suffers death or injury through political risk, preserve morale and reputation in unstable terrain, nor protect us against the failure to achieve our strategic objectives. Other political risk management measures can protect these less tangible assets, and we have an opportunity to proactively structure all relevant measures towards holistic business resilience.

POLITICAL RISK MANAGEMENT AND GLOBAL CORPORATE CITIZENSHIP

The most critical, often extreme leftist or religious, interpretation of an international business is that it is in it for a 'fast buck', puts profit ahead of contribution to society, and indeed regards harm to society arising from its activities as necessary 'collateral damage'. Short of this extreme characterisation, there is still a range of critiques along these lines, some of them justified given the mistakes that some companies have made in their interaction with society and political actors, and the periodic victory of greed over tempered common sense and respect for the law. In these perspectives, political risk management appears to be a cynically motivated process of justifying the firm's activities, while safeguarding the pursuit of raw profit whatever the risk to host communities and international civil society. This view has even arisen among the management of some companies which have adopted an 'us and them' attitude towards political and social actors, regarding 'non-business' considerations as an impediment to business expediency.

In fact, the reverse is a more justifiable perspective. Sound global corporate citizenship, that is, the contribution of a firm to the societies in which it operates and alignment with social values, is fundamental to political risk mitigation, and therefore to international business performance. First, as noted earlier, business operates within a framework defined by politics and social values. An 'us and them' perspective sets up untenable friction with the very terrain in which business occurs; the ground on which we stand is pervasive and unavoidable, yet ultimately sustains us if we adapt to it. Second, a valid truism of human nature is that trust underlies smooth relationships. If a company can be trusted to demonstrate reasonable respect for social values in its operating environments, then it will in turn be respected and its interests taken into account by political and social actors. Even in the absence of any other political risk management measure, respect for social values will go a considerable distance towards mitigating the risks arising from friction with non-business stakeholders.

Businesses face a contradiction. Their pursuit of profit has been deemed by the societies in which they operate to contribute to the social good: companies generate wealth for shareholders and suppliers, provide goods and services that are in demand, and provide employment and therefore livelihoods. Is a company therefore not fulfilling its social obligations just by being good at generating profit? It would seem so at a glance, since capitalism, the ideology underlying the perceived value of business, appears to be so widely accepted, especially in regions that international companies are most accustomed to.

However this ideology really never became more than just one of several prevailing ideals that define the social good, and economic value remains only one type by which the social contribution of any entity is judged. In order to align with social values, then, a company needs to look beyond the ideology which justifies its own existence, towards the wider spectrum of ideals that define the social good. These ideals can sometimes be contradictory and it is often impossible to align with all of them, but only in trying can a company keep friction with its environment to sustainable levels.

A business does indeed exist to generate profit, and necessarily makes this a high priority. But if it fails to recognise its other social obligations, then its political risk will significantly increase and performance will suffer as a result. There is, then, no contradiction between political risk management and global corporate citizenship, and indeed performance in the latter is an indispensible element of managing political risk. This is especially so in environments in which capitalism is relatively nascent or indeed subordinate to other value systems, as is the case in many emerging markets.

AN INTERNATIONAL COMPANY: POLITICAL ACTOR?

If a company needs to be aware of and manage political risk, does this mean that it is in fact a political actor? This need and should not be the case. We can draw an analogy to an individual citizen living in a large city with a high incidence of crime. This person wants to avoid becoming a victim of crime. They make themselves aware of recent trends in criminal targeting and dangerous neighbourhoods, take common sense precautions to avoid crime (such as travelling with friends in high-risk areas, or taking taxis to get through bad neighbourhoods, and so on), have the police emergency number pre-programmed into their mobile phone, and take a self-defence course to enable them to escape a rough encounter relatively unhurt. These precautions do not make the person a police officer. They are not obligated to seek out and defeat crime, nor do they directly compete against criminal interests. They do not, in that respect, become a 'player'.

Companies operating in high-risk political environments are in a similar position. They take precautions, and they build useful relationships in the context of their operations, but they need not become political actors. Their objective is to safely execute their legitimate business, and this need not extend to changing the political landscape or to adjusting prevailing ideologies to better suit foreign business interests. The presence of foreign businesses might adjust the political landscape over time, not just through investment but also inter-cultural interaction, but any one firm is there to fulfil its legitimate business interests within the parameters of ethical business standards, period. There is no need to become a political actor to achieve this.

In addition, there are good reasons to avoid becoming, or being perceived as, a political actor. Although, as noted earlier, there is still an array of perspectives on international businesses, by and large there is widespread consensus that the legitimate pursuit of profit is socially valuable, and that private companies are best positioned to undertake this pursuit. By sticking to business and avoiding over-extension into the political domain, a company can maintain a degree of political neutrality, and can thereby avoid the harsh treatment which political actors, whether state or non-state, are often subjected to by trying to influence the distribution of political authority or prevailing social values. If one considers the survival skills of an experienced government or opposition group, they are very unlike those of a private company, and most firms simply could not compete as a political stakeholder, nor would they want to be given the social expectations of a company's behaviour.

Furthermore, taking on a political role can dramatically erode the perception of a company's performance in corporate citizenship. If a company oversteps the limits of political risk management, and goes from self-resilience to actively seeking changes in its political environment, it is by most standards seeking to create an uneven playing field, and concealing a power agenda behind what seems like a thin veneer of legitimate business interests. Such behaviour can also justify and spread notions that the company is an agent of political interests which could well be antithetical to political ideals in its host communities. After all, companies have actually been used as fronts for political subversion and clandestine activities in the past.

Where do companies draw the line between making themselves resilient in the face of political risk, and becoming political actors? This is an awkward boundary, and some companies have overstepped it in the past. For example, there have been several alleged (though well documented) cases of direct corporate collusion with Western governments in the overthrow of anti-capitalist Latin American, African and Middle Eastern regimes who threatened nationalisation of foreign assets, as well as the hiring of mercenaries to militarily secure local operating environments experiencing civil war. Such cases have inevitably incurred political wrath, increased risk, and damaged reputation. So too have cases involving the bribing of political stakeholders.

The best, or perhaps most feasible, answer to where the boundary lies is that efforts to make oneself resilient while adhering to legal and ethical standards are within a firm's right and would be perceived as such, while efforts to alter the political operating environment, aside from support to legitimate peace-building initiatives, would make a company a political actor.

Companies do need to engage with their political environments and build relationships with political actors in the context of specific operations, but they must remain very sensitive to this boundary. When in doubt, a second opinion from reputable NGOs and respected donors who do not have a direct stake in the situation can be a useful cross-check. There is no easy answer, but being aware of the issue and keeping it on the radar is the best possible starting point.

BEYOND THE *SHORT GUIDE*

As the preceding chapters would indicate, political risk is a broad domain, and a short guide can only provide a top-level explanation and part of the picture. In terms of scope, this book confined itself to political risk, not emerging market risk generally. Other types of risk that typically arise in developing countries include health, cultural, infrastructure, and non-political criminality, for example. A full picture of the risks of operating in emerging markets would need to take these into account, and it would be possible to manage some of these with the same approaches applied to political risks.

We also purposefully focused more on issues most addressable through strategic and operational risk management, on the premise that these represented the principal gap in the literature. There is considerable material on financial, insurance and contractual risk management measures, and this should be explored as a corollary to this work. We also did not explicitly address enterprise risk management, which is a lively topic these days and something of a fad in business thinking and management consulting. There has been some useful research into how political risk management can be integrated into wider risk management systems, and this too bears investigation.

In terms of depth, the reader can be assured that there is much left to learn about most of the issues covered in this guide, and that there is sufficient material out there to keep the curious reader occupied.

At the end of Chapter 4 we also briefly addressed the concept of bias in assessment. Bias applies not only to assessments of political risk, but also to the wider interpretation of political risk – what it is and how it is best addressed. The Appendix, 'The Political Risk Consulting Landscape', also explains that any given sub-expertise in political risk management is open to its own interpretive biases, and these shape recommendations on the issue. The author is not exempt from bias, and in spite of a conscious effort to maintain objectivity, some bias will have slipped through. A broader reading on the subject, and careful interpretation of this work in the context of the reader's own organisational and strategic context, are strongly recommended as subsequent steps on the road to proficiency.

Appendix:
The Political
Risk Consulting
Landscape

Every company is a potential client of external consultants and advisers. The arguments for using consultants include the acquisition of rare specialist knowledge, temporarily adding to management capacity without incurring long-term overheads, and exposure to new management concepts and processes. Political risk management remains a specialist function, and as we have noted few firms have internal political risk departments. That being said, we have also seen that most companies with international experience do indeed have relevant expertise within their conventional management structures. It is likely, then, that external political risk experts will find a niche in supporting this specialist function, but that any external intervention can rest heavily on existing skills within the client organisation. There is no need for the proverbial 'army of consultants'.

The political risk advisory sector is comprised of several types of service providers. We will first examine each set's core proposition, and the strengths and weaknesses which each might manifest. Then we will look more closely at some of the general caveats that buyers need to be aware of in the acquisition of political risk management support.

We do not mention any specific firms herein as examples, for several reasons. Customer experience varies even with the same provider, service standards are still evolving, and our general characterisation is an estimated average, and will not apply to every firm in the given sub-segment. Strengths and weaknesses can be regarded as points to clarify in more detail when seeking external support, not as sweeping judgements on a given service segment.

As an initial insight, the reader should be aware of the terminology and how it is interpreted. Political risk management could well mean, depending on the provider's comfort-zone: security; insurance; due diligence investigations; Corporate Social Responsibility (CSR), and so on. Most advisories will know the term 'political risk', but will define it in their own way, relevant to their own expertise. The names of relevant functions (for example, security and CSR) can predominate in an advisory's positioning and give a hint to their real domain of added value.

Mid- to large-sized multidisciplinary political risk consultancies provide services across the political risk management spectrum, from country and project risk assessment and due diligence to on-the-ground security and crisis response. Such firms could, in theory, act as a guide along the whole path, right up to the evaluation of political risk management performance. They do indeed embody most of the relevant expertise for such a broad-based solution. In addition the larger ones have an international presence which enables them to respond to clients' overseas issues quickly and with local expertise.

There are two caveats in dealing with such firms. First, although in theory they might be capable of offering integrated political risk management solutions, in practice service integration is somewhat elusive. The different departments tend to remain specialists in their own domains, and there is not necessarily a common 'language' or top-level project management structure that binds the different services. Cross-departmental project outcomes can be somewhat disjointed. Second, while such firms grew to become capable of offering a wide array of services, they usually have roots in one or two core specialisations, often security or investigations. These tend to dominate the firm's wider interpretation of risk management, and other service areas can remain peripheral to how the firm interprets or addresses a client's issues.

Another kind of service provider is the consulting arm of insurance firms which provide political risk coverage. These offer advice about the client's risks and help to structure appropriate insurance packages. They also advise on non-insurance areas of risk management, which makes sense if we consider that the insurer's business performance suffers if clients face major loss as a result of political risk and need to cash in on a policy.

Some observers consider an insurance firm offering risk management consulting to be a conflict of interest, and regard their non-insurance services as merely up-front sales or as a way to increase the switching costs for customers. This is not an unreasonable assessment, but when we consider the fact that the resilience of a client's operations are of mutual benefit for the client and the insurer, it might seem somewhat cynical. Another, perhaps more justifiable concern would be that insurance firms, just like other kinds of advisories, will indeed have a unique and perhaps rather narrow interpretation of political risk and risk management. Those assets or risks which they do not insure, for example, will not figure prominently in their advisory services. The 'grey' areas of risk, such as the effect of an unstable environment on morale or the effect of excessive security on reputation, are often missed.

There is a strong linkage between insurance firms and another type of service provider: kidnap risk management consultancies. Kidnap (or K&R – kidnap and ransom, as it is often known) consultancies might be practices within larger multidisciplinary firms, or stand-alone boutiques. They support clients in cases of kidnapping or related forms of extortion, with the aim of safe release and ransom minimisation.

The typical business model is that a client will identify kidnap risk through their risk assessment and then approach an insurer to cover the risk for relevant categories of personnel. K&R insurance covers the cost of any necessary ransom and personal life insurance payouts and liabilities that could come from death or injury in kidnap cases. Importantly it also covers the services of K&R specialists retained by the insurance firm to act on behalf of its clients, and the buyer's agreement to use the retained consultants is often a requirement for obtaining the insurance. This model is a workable one. The client benefits from access to specialist K&R expertise which increases the chances of safe crisis resolution, and the insurer benefits from lower ransoms and decreased probability of having to make other related insurance payouts.

It is of course possible to gain access to K&R specialists without having to buy kidnap insurance, but often K&R firms will prioritise cases initiated by their insurance firm customers, and as rare specialists in a high-stakes domain, K&R consultants can be expensive, especially if a kidnap case drags on for several weeks or months.

Some might argue that with competent law enforcement, there is no need for K&R consultants. That might be true in Western Europe and other developed regions with relatively strong governance and professional law enforcement agencies, but in many developing regions weak governance and low professionalism can make reliance on police forces for K&R resolution very risky. In the worst cases, corrupt elements of the police might well be in collusion with the kidnappers. K&R consultants are experts at interpreting the competency of law enforcement in diverse regions, and at working with the relevant agencies to ensure that they understand and comply with global best practice in resolving cases.

In dealing with best-practice K&R firms there are few caveats; this is an area where the best firms are probably some of the most professional and discrete consultants in the world. The principal caveat would instead lie in the selection of the service provider. In addition to the top-tier, there are inevitably some firms which lack the full range of unique competencies required for the discretion, complexity and inter-cultural sensitivity in international cases. In considering K&R insurance, a prospective client should conduct reasonable due diligence on the retained K&R consultancy to ensure that they offer the best possible support.

Another common type of service provider in political risk management is country risk analysis advisories, which might be part of a multidisciplinary firm or a standalone company. Such firms are often the ones most closely associated with 'political risk' as a label. Their services involve regular country risk assessments and monitoring, and tailored risk assessments for specific client operations. Most such firms offer regular publications which allow clients to minimise their own in-house resources dedicated to political risk assessment, and to have access to the knowledge of analysts with in-depth knowledge of specific countries or regions.

Chapter 4 makes it clear that political assessment can be an extensive endeavour, and the average international company would probably not want to carry the overheads of a permanent risk analysis department, aside a small core team attached to the political risk leadership function. Reliance on country risk analysis advisories can be more cost effective, not just because they are a variable cost, but because they have the time and resources to obtain very detailed insights on specific operating environments.

There are a couple of caveats in using country risk analysis firms. First, many such firms were started and are staffed by academics or ex-government intelligence analysts. They might know international and regional politics well, but their understanding of business imperatives and operations can be quite top-level. Especially in bespoke assessments, it can be challenging for business clients to draw actionable insights from often unwieldy academic outputs. Second, in a similar vein, some such advisories do not make much use of analytical frameworks and modelling, preferring nuanced interpretive prose instead. Frameworks and models can be a very useful way for busy managers to get their heads around complex issues quickly, and to readily see the logical relationship between facts, conclusions and recommendations. This has been long understood by the strategy consulting profession, but it has yet to sink in among many country risk analysts, again partly because of the lack of background in business.

CSR consultants are another service provider, and unlike other kinds of political risk advisories they are unlikely to be found in multidisciplinary firms. CSR firms advise on how to tailor CSR programmes for increased acceptance of an international firm at the global and operational level. They are specialists in socio-environmental impact assessments, general CSR programming, and in some cases in specialist areas such as conflict sensitivity. CSR advisories often draw on experience from the NGO and donor domain, and usefully apply this to help companies to align with international development imperatives and to bridge the gap between the public/civil society and private sector perspectives.

As with most political risk-related consultancies, a caveat in dealing with these firms is sometimes their narrow interpretation of the issues. A CSR consultancy might have little understanding of the 'harder' side of risk management, such as security or K&R, or how these areas and CSR can be integrated for holistic approaches to political risk. Those firms with a strong background in the public sector or NGOs might indeed be somewhat disdainful of harder risk management measures, and can perceive experts in security in particular with some degree of wariness. Their support should be carefully guided by the client with an eye to their contribution to the wider political risk management strategy.

There is an array of small to mid-sized security consultancies outside of multidisciplinary firms, many with propositions aimed at security for operations in unstable environments. Such firms can advise on appropriate security initiatives, and many can also directly outsource or augment the security function. Those with global offerings often draw on the experience of ex-military and security personnel with considerable exposure to unstable environments.

The principal caveats in dealing with security firms include a somewhat specialist interpretation of risk management – a security operator with decades of experience in unstable locations could have a tendency to regard security as the mainstream approach to risk, and certainly the most pragmatic. Just as CSR people sometimes regard security experts with suspicion, security people can regard the 'softer' side of risk management as peripheral and in the worst cases as a public relations exercise lacking substantive benefits. Again, the client needs to guide security experts' inputs to ensure alignment with the risk management strategy and other relevant risk management functions.

Another issue in using security providers, which we discussed in Chapter 5, is the risk of obtrusive or heavy-handed security. The ideal supplier for security support in unstable regions should have a discrete and unobtrusive approach, be thoroughly versed in and compliant with the Voluntary Principles on Security and Human Rights, and able to train relevant local government security forces in compliance with the Principles. They should also be culturally sensitive, and capable of creating smooth working relationships with relevant government agencies.

Investigation firms are another common feature of the political risk management landscape. They are often found as part of multidisciplinary firms or as a department in security consultancies, but there are many stand-alone suppliers. Their services in the political risk context are primarily due diligence to ascertain the real affiliations and intentions of stakeholders with whom the company plans to associate in an overseas operation, and to detect any vested interests that could create risk for the client.

The best performers in the context of international political risk have extensive overseas networks of partners and sources to draw upon for detailed local insights, and an in-house team who are adept in the acquisition of sensitive information while adhering to legal and ethical principles, and client confidentiality. Such firms draw on backgrounds that range from government intelligence to investigative journalism and forensic accounting, and operate in multidisciplinary teams. They typically do not create detailed recommendations, but focus instead on hitting the intelligence requirement on the head in terms of facts and interpretation.

Prospective clients need to be aware of the difference between truly global providers who are familiar with the complex global operating environment, and more domestic players for whom international work is an exotic peripheral domain. Suppliers should have track records for discretion and compliance with ethical standards in their investigative work. There have been a few embarrassing incidents involving the public disclosure of investigations which relied on dubious means to obtain intelligence, with consequent reputational fallout for the supplier and its client. While this is an occupational hazard for firms in this business, such incidents should be few and far between.

Another type of service provider, or practice in a multidisciplinary firm, worthy of note are those which support personnel travelling in potentially unstable environments. These firms provide an extension of the Human Resources function as it relates to duty of care for international personnel. The typical supplier will offer travel tracking services (knowing where people are at any given moment and their status and contact details), travel security intelligence and training, evacuation services for either individual personnel with medical or other emergencies or for entire expatriate teams trapped in a worsening environment, and local emergency response in terms of medical support and in some cases also security.

The business model for engaging such firms can be similar to the use of K&R consultants, whereby the insurance provider will have retained a specialist supplier to which the client will have access as part of the policy. However, it is also possible to retain such services directly without an insurance intermediary.

Prospective clients need to be aware of the different service levels among such firms. Some, for example, might claim a global response capability when in practice their access to certain regions is constrained and it would take considerable time to tend to local emergencies. Their logistics should be straightforward and efficient. For example, it makes little sense to be able to quickly evacuate someone with a medical emergency if the ill person needs to be flown several thousand miles to one of the few hospitals with which the supplier has a partnership.

The final sub-segment which we will examine here is political risk strategy consultancies. These are perhaps the least common of the various providers. Such firms understand business strategy and political risk in detail, and are capable of guiding clients in the development of a political risk management strategy aligned to corporate and operational business imperatives. Firms in this sector tend to be boutique consultancies drawing on backgrounds in international strategy consulting or government service. They are not necessarily experts in specialist risk management functions, but they understand enough to know what sub-elements would be necessary in the definition of a risk management strategy for a given context. They are also familiar with the wider risk management industry and can help clients to negotiate the labyrinth of different propositions in sourcing the right expertise for a holistic approach to political risk.

Political risk strategy advisers should be capable of bridging the language of political risk and more conventional business functions and issues, and if they were to directly lead an engagement towards risk management strategy development, should be able to back up their top-level understanding of regions and risk management elements with access to well developed specialist networks. The client will need to look for that rare integration of business strategy and political risk know-how in order to find an effective strategic level adviser.

We have considered some of the strengths and weaknesses of the various political risk management suppliers and how they can augment risk management capability. Now we will briefly summarise some of the broader guidelines in how to maximise value from engaging with external political risk-related services in general.

First, we need to bear in mind that although political risk might seem like a niche or specialist domain in relation to more mainstream business functions, as we have noted most international firms are actually well equipped to support the political risk management strategy. External support should be acquired only as needed to plug gaps in capacity and expertise, not as an effort to outsource political risk management. The latter risks alienating people from the risk management function since few managers like to be affected by decisions made by consultants without having been an integral part of the decision-making process. It also misses the opportunity to develop internal skills in political risk management, and to extend people's comfort zones beyond their routine business functions.

Second, it is apparent from the above descriptions that many potential suppliers in this arena have unique backgrounds which will shape their interpretation of political risk, and not all have a particularly business-centric perspective. It is up to the client to carefully define what they need and when necessary to provide guidance to suppliers to ensure that their work is relevant to the client's business issues. The client also needs to shape external inputs such that the various deliverables coherently fit into the firm's integrated approach to political risk. Political risk strategy firms (and ideally top-level project managers in multidisciplinary firms) can advise in this respect, but their inputs too will need to be carefully scoped.

Finally, given the sensitivity of political risk, suppliers need to be held to the highest standards of business ethics and transparency. Confidentiality and discretion are natural to many firms in this sector, but this also creates room for a lack of transparency and in the worst cases the assumption that ethical slips will go unnoticed. In any security solution involving the potential use of force, clients need to be doubly vigilant in ensuring that they pick reputable suppliers and keep a strong eye on their comportment and compliance with relevant ethical standards.

Index